D1591953

Talking to the Stars

BOBBIE WYGANT'S
70 YEARS IN TELEVISION

Talking
to the *Stars*

To Joan Trew
Enjoy!
Bobbie Wygant

BOBBIE WYGANT

Foreword by
BOB SCHIEFFER

TCU Press

Fort Worth, Texas

Copyright © 2018 by Bobbie Wygant

Library of Congress Cataloging-in-Publication Data

Names: Wygant, Bobbie, 1926- author.
Title: Talking to the stars : Bobbie Wygant's seventy years in television /
   Bobbie Wygant.
Description: Fort Worth, Texas : TCU Press, [2018]
Identifiers: LCCN 2018020249 | ISBN 9780875656915 (alk. paper)
Subjects: LCSH: Wygant, Bobbie, 1926- | Television journalists--Biography. |
   WBAP-TV (Television station : Fort Worth, Tex.)--History--20th century. |
   Television talk shows--Texas--Fort Worth--History--20th century. |
   Interviewing on television.
Classification: LCC PN4874.W94 T35 2018 | DDC 070.92 [B] --dc23
LC record available at https://urldefense.proofpoint.com/v2/url?u=https-3A__lccn.loc.
gov_2018020249&d=DwIFAg&c=7Q-FWLBTAxn3T_E3HWrzGYJrC4RvUoWDrzTlitGRH_A&r=O2eiy819IcwTGuw-
vrBGiVdmhQxMh2yxeggw9qlTUDE&m=f_mHMYOwMrwDNCVrKJIGS89TfPgZ9yxI6WHcov1whB8&s=V_4U0CyGw
cUNSf3wNIytxOzpTVsjFXfHAK5MLMPvpZI&e=

TCU Box 298300
Fort Worth, Texas 76129
www.prs.tcu.edu

To order books: 1.800.826.8911

Cover and text design by Bill Brammer
www.fusion29.com

Photo editor: Christina Patoski

To Phil
"Leader"
the joy and love of my life

ABOVE
With a little help from *Bonanza's* Dan
Blocker (left) and Lorne Greene, I
grew to match them in height.

Foreword

Bobbie Wygant is the best example I know of what makes good local journalism—she is accurate, knows how to tell a good story, knows what is important to her community, and has earned the trust of her viewers—and all that shines through in this collection of her wonderful memories of a long career.

Bobbie was a collector of stories, and forgive me, but my favorite was one involving me. Had it not been for Bobbie, my long career in television journalism might never have happened, nor would I have ever met the most important person in my life. More on that person later, but first the part about TV.

In 1965, Bobbie had a noon talk show on WBAP-TV, the NBC affiliate in my home town, Fort Worth, and I was the night police reporter at the *Fort Worth Star-Telegram*. I made $115 a week, worked from 6:00 p.m. to 2:00 a.m., and I thought it was the best job in the world. I was doing what I had wanted to do since I was thirteen years old—be a newspaper reporter. I loved the job, but I was getting antsy. There was a war that seemed to be getting bigger in Vietnam, a far-off place that most of us couldn't find on a map. I convinced the *Star-Telegram* editors to send me there to cover it.

My assignment was to find as many kids from Texas as I could and write stories about them. Their friends and relatives sent me eight hundred letters, and using the letters to track them down, I found 220 of them.

Finding those young people who were so far from home and lonely was the most rewarding experience I ever had. The circulation of the *Star-Telegram* went up seven thousand subscribers, and when I returned to Fort Worth in the spring of 1966, I found I was something of a local celebrity. It seemed that every service club and church group in Fort Worth invited me to speak.

Alas, I soon discovered my fame had not spread beyond Texas. On the plane home from Vietnam, I had decided I wanted to work for a national newspaper, and I bombarded the *New York Times*, the *Washington Post,* and all the big publications with résumés, news clippings of my work, and requests for job interviews. I had realized in Vietnam that TV employed real reporters, so I also sent résumés to the networks as well.

Except for *Life* Magazine and a Houston television station which was looking for an investigative reporter and said it made no difference that I lacked TV experience, no one seemed interested in my job applications.

Enter Bobbie Wygant. She called one day and invited me to be on her noon interview show with instructions to bring along my Vietnam photos.

I did as directed, and two days later I was stunned when the news director at WBAP, our local NBC television affiliate, called and asked if I would be interested in anchoring their 6:00 and 10:00 p.m. newscasts! He said Vietnam had become such a big story, and my experience there would make up for the on-camera television experience I lacked. After seeing me on Bobbie Wygant's show, he thought I would catch on fast to how TV worked. It meant I would be leaving the *Star-Telegram*, staying in Fort Worth, and not working at the national level. Nothing lost there—no national publication had offered me a job, and the WBAP job paid twenty dollars a week more than I was making at the paper, so I took it.

Over the years I have often wondered where I would be today had Bobbie not given me the "audition" that led to that job.

But that's just the half of it. Because I had chosen to stay in Fort Worth, I was sitting in the WBAP newsroom a few months later when I got a call from George Ann Carter, wife of the *Star-Telegram* publisher Amon Carter Jr. I hardly knew the woman, and was stunned when she inquired about my marital status. When I responded that I had never been married, she said, "Then I want you to meet my next-door neighbor; how about Sunday afternoon at our house?"

Because it was the publisher's wife, the following Sunday I drove to the Carter house and was introduced to Pat Penrose. Three weeks later we decided to get married, officially tied the knot three months after our introduction, and on April 15, 2018, celebrated our fifty-first anniversary.

Bobbie has dozens upon dozens of stories like that in this book. She's not only a great storyteller—she's got the pictures!

One more thing: thank you, Bobbie!

—Bob Schieffer

ONE

Destiny

Working in television was my destiny. Working for NBC was also preordained. It all started in 1939. I was twelve years old. That summer my grandparents, Robert E. and Anne Connolly, took me to the New York World's Fair.

OPPOSITE
The RCA Exhibit Building at the 1939 New York World's Fair featured an experimental television receiver encased in a Lucite cabinet to display its inner workings.

We also toured RCA's headquarters at Rockefeller Center. The main attraction was the new experimental television studio where visitors could talk in front of a TV camera. My grandfather was an uninhibited cutup who jumped at the chance to experience this new phenomenon and to broadcast to spectators on the other side of the makeshift studio and perhaps to a few people in New York City who owned home television sets.

When Granddad was finished he gently pushed me in front of the camera. I said, "My name is Roberta Connolly. I'm from Lafayette, Indiana. I'm twelve years old and will be in the eighth grade." I was on a roll, so I told the live camera that besides New York we went to Boston, where my Granddad attended a Postal Supervisors Convention. Granddad was in charge of the post office in Lafayette. There's no permanent record of my inauspicious broadcast debut. Videotape was decades away,

but in future years there would be volumes of kinescopes, films, and tapes of me on air.

The New York appearance was my debut on live television—and on network TV yet. I started at the top. Little could I have imagined then that I would make a career of it and spend seventy years of my life working at the same television station in Dallas-Fort Worth.

The New York City trip was exhilarating on another level. I was becoming more and more interested in the entertainment business—not in being an actress or performer, but being a part of the action. When "Mamah" and Granddad announced we would be going to see the new movie, *The Wizard of Oz*, with a stage show featuring Judy Garland and Mickey Rooney, I was about to explode with excitement. Judy Garland and Mickey Rooney LIVE IN PERSON! Wow! This is the same twelve-year-old who would one day grow up and sit in front of a TV camera to talk with Mickey Rooney.

ABOVE
The Radio Corporation of America (RCA) was developing radios that also received television pictures. Fairgoers flocked to see the revolutionary television set displayed at the World's Fair RCA Building. This was the first time most people had seen a TV.

LEFT
Visitors to the RCA Building lined up to be televised live in front of a TV camera at the telemobile unit. Television was still in its infancy, broadcasting just a few hours a week to very small viewing areas where there were only a tiny number of receivers.

ABOVE

RCA gave out cards at the Fair to those who spoke in front of the TV camera to commemorate their television debut.

ABOVE

The ghost TV at the World's Fair displayed a television picture which was a mirror reflection of the electronic cathode ray tube located in the cabinet. Viewers looked at the tube's reflection in a mirror attached to the inside of the cabinet lid.

Courtesy Hagley Museum and Library.

RIGHT

The early TV sets were built inside tall wooden cabinets to accommodate the large vertical cathode ray tubes. The TV cabinets, described by some as "radio with pictures," closely resembled the radios of the 1930s that families typically sat around to listen together to favorite nightly radio programs.

From a very early age my mother, Nellie Connolly (née Ella Louise Toner) from Indianapolis, saw that my two brothers and I were exposed to the arts. She read classic stories to us at bedtime. We had dance lessons, mostly tap, and music lessons. For me, it was a steel guitar. Gordon, the middle child, had accordion lessons. But Carl, the youngest, preferred storytelling.

The first movie I remember seeing with my mother was *Wings*. It was released in 1927 but didn't see general release until 1929. I was three years old. *Wings* won the first Academy Award in 1929 for what was then called "Outstanding Picture" and won another award for "Outstanding Engineering Effects." Today that award would be Visual Effects. *Wings* was a

silent film with a musical score, but it must have been very realistic, because my three-year-old mind freaked out. I can remember the airplanes flying off the screen directly at me. I don't know if I made a scene, but I remember it scared the bejabbers out of me. For the longest time I refused to see any movie that had airplanes in it. Fast forward to the 1960s and beyond, when most weekends I flew someplace in the USA—and often abroad—to interview film stars, racking up over two million miles each with both American and Delta Airlines.

I started talking to stars before I was a teenager. Clyde McCoy, a trumpet player noted for his rendition of "Sugar Blues," was doing a stage show between movie showings at the Mars Theater. My two brothers and I, dressed in

ABOVE LEFT
My New York trip was a life-changing event for an impressionable preteen.

ABOVE
The Wizard of Oz broke house records when it premiered in New York City at Loew's Capitol Theatre on Broadway in August 1939. Nearby streets around the theater were closed because of the crowds. Judy Garland, who was not the studio's first choice for Dorothy, sang and danced live with her Andy Hardy cohort Mickey Rooney on the Loew's stage between film showings—sometimes as many as nine shows a day.

ABOVE LEFT AND CENTER
I was Nellie and Loren Connolly's first child.

ABOVE FAR RIGHT
Mother enjoyed taking me and my brother Gordon on nature outings.

RIGHT
Gordon (left) and Carl (right) were my two younger brothers. We were all close in age and became constant companions.

FAR RIGHT
I received my first communion in 1932 at St. Lawrence Catholic Church in Lafayette, Indiana. I attended Catholic schools for all twelve grades.

ABOVE
I was always among the smallest and youngest in my class, but I managed to stay on the honor roll and was active socially. I was never shy about public speaking.

ABOVE
Big band leader Clyde McCoy was a popular trumpet player who toured nationally for decades. He was best known for his hit recording of "Sugar Blues," which became his theme song. In July 1942, *DownBeat* magazine featured him and his backup singers, the Bennett Sisters, on its cover. Today, his name lives on in the music world with the Clyde McCoy Cry Baby Wah Pedal, an electronic guitar effect named after his trademark quivering trumpet sound.

RIGHT
Another photo from my
high school days. There was
a time in high school when
I aspired to be a doctor.

ABOVE

The Purdue Hall of Music opened in 1940 and immediately became a world-class venue for national touring companies, from the Metropolitan Opera to the Ballet Russe de Monte Carlo. Located on the Purdue college campus, it is one of the largest proscenium theaters in the US. Designed by Walter Scholer, with assistance from J. Andre Fouilhoux, who was one of the architects for Radio City Music Hall in New York, the hall seats six thousand. WBAA radio studios, where I had my first hands-on broadcasting experiences, are located in the basement of the hall. It was renamed the Elliott Hall of Music in 1958.

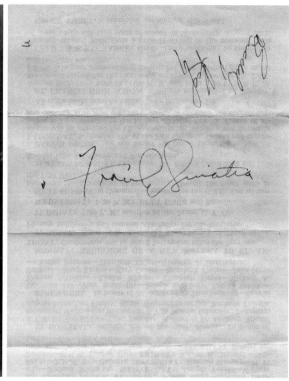

ABOVE RIGHT
I loved popular music, with Frank Sinatra at the top of my list. I saw him perform with the Tommy Dorsey band every chance I had, even traveling by bus to Indianapolis.

ABOVE FAR RIGHT
I tracked down Frank Sinatra at his hotel, where I got him and Buddy Rich to sign their autographs on the back of my church bulletin.

our Easter outfits, got down-front seats. During an audience participation McCoy selected me to come on stage to lead his orchestra. I think my brother Gordon was embarrassed, but I loved it. Gordon liked it better when McCoy took us for sodas after the show.

Purdue University, located across the Wabash River in West Lafayette, had regular programs for schoolchildren, everything from the Indianapolis Symphony to Ballet Russe de Monte Carlo to the Metropolitan Opera on tour. My first opera was *Carmen*, starring the famous Rise Stevens. Years later I remember sharing this memory during an interview with the renowned tenor Luciano Pavarotti. Purdue's Elliott Hall of Music is a world-class state-of-the-art venue that seats six thousand and is considered a sister to Radio City Music Hall. Both halls share the same designer. One could stand in the second balcony and carry on a conversation with someone on stage in a

normal voice.

I loved the classical arts but I was also a bobby soxer. This was a nickname in the 1940s attached to teenage girls who wore ankle socks and were avid fans of certain popular male singers. Frank Sinatra probably had the biggest coterie of bobby soxers.

I read *DownBeat* magazine religiously and loved the big bands. When I was thirteen, my girl friends and I would ride the bus to Indianapolis to see the stars. Once when Sinatra was singing with Tommy Dorsey I found out which hotel they were in. I bribed a bellman (if you can call fifteen cents a bribe) to give me Sinatra's room number. I wanted an autograph, but no one answered my knock or the room phone. I wondered if the bellman gave me the right room number. Not to worry. We went to the stage door between shows and got his autograph—as well as many autographs of his band members.

FAR LEFT
Sweet sixteen portrait. I started using the nickname "Bobbie" while attending St. Francis High School, an all-female convent academy run by Franciscan nuns.

LEFT
Me with my mother and aunt Jeanne Toner (center) on a special trip to Indianapolis.

OPPOSITE TOP
In high school, I was involved in a lot of extracurricular activities, including plays. Here I am (fourth from left), starring as Peg in the comedy *Three Pegs*.

OPPOSITE LEFT
In addition to school work and after-school activities, my senior year was challenging because I helped my father, now a single parent, to cook, clean, and take care of my two younger brothers.

OPPOSITE RIGHT
My Girl Scout troop volunteered to be museum aides at the Tippecanoe County Historical Museum. In this photo I'm just left of center.

Another time the Tommy Dorsey band was playing at Purdue, a high-school girl friend and I went to the Fowler Hotel in downtown Lafayette and hung out in the lobby hoping to see Sinatra and Buddy Rich, the drummer. When they came through the lobby, we stopped them. They were very nice and signed autographs. I still have the signatures, which they wrote on the back of our Sunday church bulletins. Lucky for me, celebrities did not intimidate me.

Life was good my first three years in high school. I was an honor student, and my social life was fun. But tragedy was lurking in the shadows. My carefree life was about to come to an end.

Before the broadcasting bug bit me, I thought I wanted to be a doctor. I met a couple of times with a female doctor in Lafayette. We talked about her career as a general practitioner and about her family life. She was married to a doctor who was an eye, ear, nose, and throat specialist. The nearest medical school was Indiana University in Bloomington, the southern part of Indiana. Though I realized that it would be a financial burden on my parents to go away to school, I was serious about wanting to be a doctor.

So what changed my mind? Early in 1943 my mother became ill with what was diagnosed as strep throat. When it lingered, she went to a specialist. She was found to have malignant nasal polyps. For many years she was bothered with hay fever and allergies. To treat the malignant polyps she underwent

ROBERTA CONNOLLY
"Bobbie"
Sinatra fan
"Oh Johnny"

X-ray and radium treatments. The specialist who treated her was married to the female doctor with whom I had had career talks. Mother's condition kept deteriorating, and she died in September 1943—one week before I was to start my senior year in high school. She was thirty-seven.

Mother's death had a profound effect on our family. It was the middle of World War II, and domestic help was not available. Almost everyone who could work but didn't get drafted was employed in the defense industry. My dad was employed by the post office and was a single parent, so he was exempt. He worked nights, so I helped him keep house and cook for the family.

Losing Mother turned me away from medicine as a career. I was just sixteen, and

my mother had just died. I didn't think I would ever be able to cope with patients dying.

About this time I discovered Purdue University's radio station WBAA. What caught my attention was that the station had female announcers. They did the same kinds of programs the guys did. I specifically remember listening to Becky Ann Purvine, who was a local girl. Since I was good at public speaking, I thought maybe I should consider broadcasting.

Granddad was friends with one of the deans at Purdue. He arranged a meeting, and the dean said with my high grades I could enter Purdue in the fall and start working toward a major in broadcasting. But first I had to finish high school.

ABOVE LEFT
Thirty-six women were in my high school senior class. The class prophecy entry in my yearbook read: "Roberta Connolly is now dean of women at the University of California. She's a little older, but she's still swooning over Frankie."

ABOVE RIGHT
Me on high school graduation day June 4, 1944, with my father, Loren.

RIGHT
As soon as I arrived on the Purdue campus, I went directly to the WBAA radio station to apply to be on the student staff. After classes, I spent all my time at the station and was almost immediately put on mic.

Nine months later, my father remarried. His new wife had a son the age of my youngest brother. I'm sure my father had the best interests at heart for me and my brothers, but the two families did not blend well. For a while it looked like I would not be going to college. But my grandparents, who lived close to the Purdue campus, came to the rescue. They insisted I come live with them, and they would pay my tuition at Purdue. I am eternally grateful to them.

My father's marriage was on and off. When Gordon finished high school he joined the navy, and Carl joined the army. I entered Purdue in November 1944 and got my BS in broadcasting two years and seven months later. I lacked only three hours for a double major in psychology. My final semester I carried twenty-three hours and made the honor roll. It's not that I had a genius IQ. I just worked my buns off. Remember this expression. It will come up later in one of

my most memorable interviews.

If working in broadcasting and television was my destiny, working in Texas was also to be my destiny. From an early age I was attracted to Texas. I remember an Olivia de Havilland western where she was working in an orchard in Texas. I loved the look of Texas. In the fifth grade at St. Boniface Elementary School, we had to do a special project on one of the forty-eight states. I was the first to volunteer. I wanted to do Texas. I got a big map of Texas and pasted on pictures of cattle and oil wells and cowboys. I wrote a paper extolling the advantages of Texas and got an A on the project. On the trip to New York with my grandparents in 1939, our group included people from other states. I enjoyed hanging out with the Texans. They were very friendly, and I loved their accents.

Attending Purdue was the link that would get me to Texas. One of the first things I did after signing up for classes as a freshman was

ABOVE LEFT
Phil Wygant (on left) with Dick Fraser (middle) and Frank Baird-Smith, who were all on the WBAA student staff. Fraser and I once reported live for WBAA from a Purdue basketball game. At halftime Fraser left the booth, leaving me to fill the air for more than fifteen minutes with nothing happening on the floor. It was my first time to report at a sports event. And my last.

ABOVE RIGHT
WBAA radio went on the air in 1922, giving it the distinction of being Indiana's oldest continuously operating radio station. Programming ran from educational programs and symphony concerts to sports, children's programs, and playing records.

RIGHT
Phil (far right) was
instrumental in starting
Purdue's chapter of the
broadcasting honor society,
Alpha Epsilon Rho. His Texas
traveling buddy, Wallis "Tex"
McCormick, is fifth from right.
I am third from left.

to go to WBAA, Purdue's radio station. WBAA had a professional staff as well as a student staff. They had me do an on-air audition and write introductions to a couple of programs. They put me on the student staff. When I wasn't in classes, I worked at the radio station.

WBAA is the oldest continuously operating radio station in Indiana, dating back to experimental radio in 1910 and receiving its first broadcasting license in 1922. Its sports coverage is legendary. Today the station is a National Public Radio affiliate broadcasting news, classical music, opera, jazz, and educational programs on three separate frequencies on the radio dial.

One day there was a call for a student to do "color" commentary for a basketball game to be broadcast that weekend. I had not done any sports coverage, so I quickly volunteered. The play-by-play guy was a student, Dick Fraser. He assisted the staff sportscaster, Johnny DeCamp, known as the "Voice of Purdue" for forty-four years.

When halftime came, Fraser took off his headset and left the booth. I was alone to do thirty minutes of "color." After fifteen minutes, I had exhausted all of my prepared material. I couldn't get down from the booth to snare interviews. There was nothing happening on the floor. But I talked and talked and talked. Just as I was describing the red, white, and blue bunting decorating the gym, Fraser reappeared. I could have clobbered him. That was the beginning and end of my sports broadcasting career.

Even during the war years, Purdue's ratio of men to women was six men to every woman. At the radio station I was one of three female students studying broadcasting. The girls never lacked for dates. The older students helped us newcomers. I noticed one guy who was looked up to by all the students. He was always organizing something. He was even good at organizing picnics. He helped bring Alpha Epsilon Rho, the Broadcasting Honorary Honor Society, to Purdue. One day he came to me

ABOVE LEFT
Phil (left) supervised a WBAA popular music program
I wrote and presented. The assistant manager of
WBAA oversaw both of us. WBAA provided a solid foundation
for our future lives as broadcasters.

ABOVE RIGHT
I received my bachelor of science in broadcasting in 1947,
earning it in less than three years. I took on a twenty-three-
hour load my last semester at Purdue to get there.

LEFT
Phil and I were members of the 920 Club, made up of
students who worked at WBAA, which broadcast at 920
on the radio dial. We became engaged in September 1946
and began plans for a June 1947 wedding.

ABOVE
After graduating, I had just a couple of weeks before my wedding and the big move to Texas in the summer of 1947.

with an idea for an afternoon music program. I was already writing the script each day for the afternoon Symphony Hour. This new program would feature popular music, both old and new. I was to produce, write, and read the on-air introductions. He would be my supervisor. His name was Phil Wygant, and he came from South Bend, Indiana.

Phil was pleasant but all business at the station. He was different in class. I remember a history class where the professor said we could sit wherever we liked. Being small I sat up front where I could see the blackboard. This Phil Wygant came and sat next to me. One day when I looked back at my notebook, he had written in big letters FOO. I had no idea what that meant, so I flipped to a clean page and ignored him. Several classes later when I was watching the professor, I turned to write a note and again the page was filled with FOO.

After class I said, "Why do you write FOO all over my notebook?"

He said, "Don't you read the funny papers?"

I replied, "Not very much."

He looked puzzled and said, "Well look at Smokey Stover and you'll see what FOO is all about."

It meant nothing. It was a running gag in the strip with FOO appearing any place for no reason. I still don't get it.

In addition to classes and his radio station duties, Phil did stage work for Purdue's Hall of Music. He had studied theater lighting at South Bend's Central High School, the same school movie director Sydney Pollack attended. The International Alliance of Theatrical Stage Employees (IATSE) in Lafayette didn't have enough members to staff some of the national touring shows Purdue booked, so qualified students filled in. Phil earned union wages but did not have to join the union. During this time he worked under famous New York lighting directors, among them Jo Mielziner, winner of seven Tony Awards for stage and lighting design.

FOO writer Phil and I were friends, but we did not date. I joined Alpha Xi Delta sorority and was dating different guys. Then one day in June 1945 Phil asked me for a date. The next thing I knew we were going steady. He gave me a ring in September 1946, and we set the wedding date for June 28, 1947, the date of my grandparents' forty-eighth wedding anniversary.

Phil graduated from Purdue in February of 1947. A fellow classmate, Wallis "Tex" McCormick, asked Phil to join him on his trip back to Texas. Phil could help him with the long drive to Fort Worth, where Tex would visit his fiancée Martha Ingram. It was February, which meant warm, shirtsleeve weather in Texas. Phil had never been west of Chicago. February in Indiana was usually snow up to your knees. Texas was heaven!

While Phil didn't think a large market like Dallas-Fort Worth would hire a newly graduated broadcasting major, Tex urged him to look for a job. Phil went to KXOL, the smallest radio station. The manager auditioned him and said, "I would hire you now but I have no openings. Let me make a phone call." He called Frank Mills, the chief announcer at WBAP, a fifty-thousand-watt clear channel radio station. Phil auditioned for Frank Mills and was offered a staff announcer job. Phil called me and said, "Do you think you'd like living in Texas?" I said, "If that's where you're going to be, I'll like it fine."

My Texas connection was made!

TWO

WBAP-TV Signs On

Our wedding was Saturday morning, June 28, 1947, at St. Boniface Catholic Church in Lafayette, Indiana. Phil was twenty-one. I was twenty.

OPPOSITE
Philip Wygant and I exchanged vows in Indiana on June 28, 1947, and arrived in Texas two days later.

My grandparents, Robert and Anne Connolly, hosted the wedding, the bridal party breakfast following the wedding, and the afternoon reception for friends and relatives. I had one attendant, Doris Burkle, a close pal from elementary and high school. Phil's best man was a high school buddy, Henry "Hank" Froning. The ushers were Purdue classmates.

We took the train to Chicago that evening and spent the night there. On Sunday we boarded another train, and by Monday we were in Texas. My first impression was *Shut the oven door!* It was so hot. Mind you, our wedding on June 28 in Indiana was the first warm day we had had that year. Homes did not have air conditioning at that time in Indiana. Only theaters and public buildings had air conditioning. Our apartment on Fort Worth's south side had window units called evaporative coolers—a far cry from air conditioning, but better than nothing. Welcome to Texas!

WBAP had applied for a license to start a TV station in 1946, although the employees weren't privy to the plans at that point. A few years later, the story emerged that Amon Carter Sr., founder and publisher of the *Fort Worth Star-Telegram* and owner of WBAP Radio, wanted to get high ground on which to build a TV transmitter for his TV station. High ground would get a better signal. So his people went looking and found high ground on the east side of Fort Worth in what is called

LEFT
Carter Publications applied to the FCC in April 1946 for a construction permit for a television station. Ground was broken for the building in February 1947 with orders to build a plant that would be the finest in the Southwest.

Meadowbrook. They reported their finding to Mr. Carter, who raised his voice and said, "Well, find out who owns it!"

They triumphantly cried, "You do, Mr. Carter. You do!"

A follow-up story is related by the award-winning journalist and *Star-Telegram* reporter, Jerry Flemmons. In his 1978 biography of Amon Carter called *Amon*, Flemmons recalls that Carter and Harold Hough, the *Star-Telegram* circulation manager, went to see

the high-ground property. In the early days of WBAP Radio, Hough was also the on-air personality who called himself "The Hired Hand." Hough, who had lost part of a leg in a train accident when he was a child, was for years the station's only announcer. Audiences loved his folksy, down-home manner and his Texas wit. When radio became more sophisticated, Hough said he was replaced by those guys with "lace on their tonsils."

RIGHT

Advertisements for the first television station in the Southwest started appearing in the summer of 1948. "A miracle is coming," is how one press release described the simultaneous sight-and-sound event that would be WBAP-TV's debut: "For the first time in this part of the country, a person living in the Fort Worth-Dallas area may soon sit in his own home, see and hear (at one and the same time) his favorite sports, music, drama, moving pictures and news as it happens."

Harold Hough was the guiding force behind WBAP radio and WBAP-TV. Through his uncanny foresight, he convinced Amon G. Carter to invest $300 in 1922 to start a radio station. At the time, Hough was the circulation manager of the *Fort Worth Star-Telegram*, the newspaper Carter owned. WBAP radio had a two-man staff when they signed on in May 1922, with Hough wearing three hats: chief engineer, announcer, and program director. The WBAP call letters stood for "We Bring A Program," suggested by Herbert Hoover, who was Secretary of Commerce in 1922. Starting as a ten-watt radio station, WBAP radio grew into a giant 50,000-watt Class A clear-channel station.

An earthy country boy at heart, Hough rarely took off his hat and had a wooden leg following a childhood accident. He developed a folksy on-air radio personality who used a cowbell as his audible punctuation trademark.

Coming Soon

WBAP

TV-DAY

STAR-TELEGRAM TELEVISION SERVICE

CHANNEL 5

ABOVE
As opening day approached, advertisements for the trail-blazing television event increased.

OPPOSITE
The new station on Broadcast Hill was located four miles east of downtown Fort Worth and twenty-six miles from Dallas. A 502-foot transmitting tower behind the building sent out a 100,000-watt signal. Because of the surrounding flat terrain, the signal reached about a forty-mile radius, from Dallas and Waxahachie to McKinney and Denton, much farther than anticipated.

ABOVE
Phil Wygant (left) joined WBAP radio as an announcer, but was more interested in getting into television production because of the theatrical lighting experience he got during his Purdue days. In the summer of 1948, he joined WBAP-TV's production crew as lighting director. He rolled up his sleeves with Bob Grammer (center) and got to work.

On the brushy Meadowbrook property Carter and Hough crawled through a barbed-wire fence to reach the high ground. Immediately Hough spotted a young bull that was giving them the once-over. Hough wanted to leave, but Carter said no, the bull wouldn't bother them. When the bull started pawing the ground, Hough turned to Carter and said, "I'm gittin' outta here. I've got a wooden leg, and that bull don't know who you are!"

By the summer of 1948, WBAP had started getting a staff together for the TV station.

Phil had wanted very much to get into TV production while he was at Purdue and was always keeping an eye out for jobs in TV. He even interviewed once at a station in Newark, New Jersey. Now Phil got the opportunity to join TV production as the lighting director for WBAP-TV. His professional experience working national shows performing at the Purdue Hall of Music paid off. He designed the lighting for the big WBAP studio and went to New York to purchase the equipment. He was twenty-two years old.

LEFT
Considered high tech for the time, the WBAP-TV field unit included three RCA TK-30A cameras for remotely televising special events and sports, especially high school and college football games. The custom-designed truck was affectionately nicknamed the Grey Goose, or alternatively the Bread Truck.

September 29, 1948, was to be WBAP-TV's official sign-on date. On September 27, however, President Harry S. Truman, campaigning for his reelection, made a whistle-stop at the Texas and Pacific Railroad Station in Fort Worth. WBAP-TV set up a remote site for what was to be a test, because the station was not yet licensed for broadcast. Amon G. Carter, however, wanted the Truman visit to be broadcast, so license or no license, it was broadcast. Before it began Mr. Carter told his son, Amon Jr., to go entertain Truman's daughter Margaret so Mr. Carter could talk with President Truman. Being a dutiful son, Amon Jr. escorted Margaret to his nearby convertible. With the Secret Service in close pursuit, Amon Jr. set out for Eagle Mountain Lake, where he gave Margaret a tour of the Carter yacht. Meanwhile, back at the T and P Building, WBAP-TV "broadcast" its first program, a campaign speech by President Truman to a live audience of several hundred people.

Two days later, on Wednesday, September 29, 1948, at 7 p.m. Frank Mills, live on camera, spoke the first official words on WBAP-TV, the first television station in the Southwest. Mills introduced Harold Hough, the *Star-Telegram* circulation manager, who was also the newly appointed general manager of WBAP-TV. Hough then presented founder Amon G. Carter Sr., who was a die-hard Fort Worth booster. When WBAP-TV debuted, however, NBC wanted it known that its programs were for both Fort Worth and Dallas.

OPPOSITE
Texas television history was made on September 27, 1948, when WBAP-TV broadcast its first pictures. Even though WBAP-TV was technically not licensed by the FCC to begin broadcasting until two days later, Channel 5 sent out its mobile field unit to downtown Fort Worth to broadcast live President Harry Truman's whistle-stop campaign speech. Never mind there were almost no television sets in homes yet.

ABOVE
Hundreds of people, including Congressman
Lyndon B. Johnson, showed up for Truman's
brief Fort Worth stop. The US Marine Band
played the national anthem. It was the first
remote telecast in Texas.

OPPOSITE
WBAP's Frank Mills and Bud Sherman did
the on-air announcing hanging off a ladder
at the top of the truck as Truman arrived
and before his thirty-minute speech.

LEFT AND ABOVE
Security held back the crowds who came to see President Truman. WBAP-TV officials considered the Truman broadcast a prelude to the official WBAP-TV Day two days later.

ABOVE
"This is WBAP-TV Fort Worth" were
the first words heard on Channel
5's inaugural broadcast from the
station on September 28, 1948.
WBAP radio's chief announcer
Frank Mills had the honors when
the station signed on at 7:00 p.m.
Mills, who joined WBAP radio as an
announcer in 1936, made an easy
transition to TV thanks to his good
looks, amiable personality, and
commanding voice. He was named
chief announcer and the host of
his own shows on both WBAP-TV
and radio.

ABOVE RIGHT
Harold Hough, the *Star-Telegram's*
vice president and director of radio
and TV, was the first person to
appear on WBAP-TV's opening night
broadcast. On the left, partially
obscured by a camera, is his
decades-long boss Amon G. Carter,
who was next up to speak.

Mr. Carter emphasized Fort Worth by promoting the station as Fort Worth/Dallas rather than the reverse. On the local level some Fort Worth viewers objected to the station reporting Dallas news. The concept of the Dallas-Fort Worth metroplex took years to achieve acceptance.

Following the introductory speeches of the first broadcast, the premiere program featured a fifteen-minute newsreel of local happenings prepared by the WBAP-TV News Department. It was silent film, with narration read live by Lillard Hill. Then a western band, The Flying X Ranch Boys, fronted a country variety show. The big finish for this first telecast to one-thousand receivers was a movie, *The Scarlet Pimpernel*, a 1935 British period piece starring Merle Oberon and Leslie Howard, the actor who played Ashley Wilkes in *Gone With the Wind*. *Pimpernel* almost got shown upside down and backwards, but the problem was caught in time to rewind the film and get it on the air. Then another problem. A truck crashed into a nearby utility pole, leaving the station without power and off the air for seventeen minutes. But hey! TV had come to Texas! As Jack Gordon of the *Fort Worth Press* wrote after he listed all the mishaps, "but TV is here to stay."

And so was I.

ABOVE LEFT

Star-Telegram and WBAP owner Amon G. Carter (center) gave welcoming remarks at the inaugural broadcast, one of the few times he appeared in public without his trademark Shady Oak cowboy hat. Seated left to right: WBAP-TV Chief Engineer R. C. "Super" Stinson, WBAP-TV Station Manager George Cranston, and Harold Hough.

ABOVE

Getting a first-hand look at the station were local and regional press representatives, including (left to right) Don McIver, *Dallas Morning News*; Amon G. Carter; Harold Hough; Frank King, Associated Press; Lee Bond, United Press International; and Al E. Stine, Associated Press. The initial investment for the station was $1.5 million, about a third of which was for the latest, top-of-the-line electronic equipment.

ABOVE

Opening night dignitaries and WBAP staff stood in the middle of Video Lane, the most unique feature of the new building. Two fifteen- by twelve-foot overhead doors on opposite sides of the TV studio could be opened directly to the outdoors. This allowed all manner of livestock, large trucks, and automobiles to drive directly into the studio and exit back outside through the door on the other side. Harold Hough requested the doors be designed to be big enough to run a herd of cattle through. Rumor was that Amon Carter wanted the doors that big so he could ride into the studio on his horse without having to get off.

ABOVE
Broadcast of the first test pattern with WBAP-TV call letters and cowbell motif started on September 15, 1948. Initially, the test pattern was broadcast with background music from 11:00 a.m. to noon and from 4:00 p.m. to 5:00 p.m. After the station officially signed on, Channel 5 broadcast about four hours of programming a night, Wednesdays through Saturdays.

ABOVE
Fort Worth's Flying X Ranch Boys (left to right: Lefty Perkins, Carrol Hubbard, Red Kidwell, leader Mel Cox, Marvin Montgomery, and barefoot Roscoe Pierce) had a popular following thanks to their weekly hit show on WBAP radio, so they were a shoo-in to perform live on WBAP-TV's first live telecast. They starred in the station's first locally sponsored and produced television variety show.

RIGHT
When the station signed on in September 1948, the WBAP building was far from finished. It was several months before the staff could move in.

THREE

Early Days at Channel 5

Phil Wygant was passing George Cranston, WBAP-TV station manager, in the hall one day not long before the station went live. Cranston said, "Doesn't your bride have a broadcasting degree?"

OPPOSITE
By May 1949, the number of TV households in the WBAP-TV viewing area had grown to 9,200, with an estimated total of 16,000 viewers.

P hil said, "Yes, from Purdue."

"Can she write?"

Phil replied that I wrote, produced, and did on-air.

"Does she want a job?" Cranston asked.

"Oh yes," Phil responded.

"Then have her call Lyman Brown in the continuity department."

The following Monday I met with Mr. Brown. He put me to work immediately. That was two weeks before WBAP-TV signed on. I like to say "they poured me in with the foundation."

The continuity department prepared a daily book that included all intros, commercials, and announcements to be made by the off-camera announcer. For several months we worked out of the WBAP radio offices on the top two floors of the Medical Arts Building in downtown Fort Worth. The new TV station building on Fort Worth's east side was the first facility in the nation built specifically for TV broadcasting. It was not completely finished when the station went on the air. The night of the official sign-on Amon Carter Sr. stepped into a hole in the studio floor that would have dropped the company's top man to the basement, had it not been for the quick action of production worker and cartoonist Johnny Hay. He reached out in time to keep Mr. Carter from doing a disappearing act.

TELEVISION

LIFE

TO A LIVELY SPANISH TUNE, A BUNCH OF FRIGHTENED CALVES IS HERDED THROUGH A TEXAS TELEVISION STUDIO. CALF AT RIGHT JUST MISSED CAMERAMAN

From the pages of LIFE

LEFT
A three-page spread in *LIFE*'s April 11, 1949, issue illustrated the station's Video Lane to dramatic effect.

LIFE and LIFE logo are registered trademarks of Time, Inc. Used under license.

TELEVISION, TEXAS STYLE

Horses and cattle cavort in Fort Worth studio to lend local color

BOOTED CAMERAMAN rides his camera with feet planted in stirrups. He says it gives him "stability."

When television hit Texas last fall, set owners within reach of the Southwest's biggest station, WBAP-TV at Fort Worth, expected something that would really spell out the Texas spirit. They got it. Outside the studio the station's well-heeled owners, Carter Publications, Inc., picked up every rodeo, stock show and cutting-horse contest within range. Inside the studio they ran chuck wagons, cow ponies, autos and an occasional elephant from a visiting circus past the cameras and regularly put on big barn dances with as many as 120 people prancing about on the huge 82-foot-long floor. To provide local color for corny standard features like the Flying X Ranchboys (*above*), once billed as the Light Crust Doughboys when they helped elect Pappy O'Daniel governor, the station director frequently runs a herd of cattle right through the studio. This sometimes allows pleased Texans to watch an alert stock handler bulldog an errant calf just before it demolishes a camera or gets badly tangled up in the studio's steel scaffolding. (It never lets them see the arrival of many "cowhands" in well-polished Cadillacs.)

The station's ordinary range, a whopping 215 miles, has given Texans something new to brag about. Although most eastern stations are happy with extreme ranges of 80 to 100 miles, gloating WBAP-TV engineers claim that because of flat terrain they can supply Texas television fare to set owners in Hattiesburg, Miss., 490 air miles away.

CONTINUED ON NEXT PAGE 151

Television sets were so expensive few people could afford them. Most people watched TV on television sets that were in bars, hotels, appliance stores, and other retail outlets where TVs were sold.

ABOVE
Channel 5's Chief Engineer R. C. "Super" Stinson (left) and engineer Rupert Bogan make adjustments to the master control console.

LEFT
Television pioneer Captain Bill Eddy (left) paid a visit to WBAP-TV Station Manager George Cranston (right) to check out the station's new RCA TK-10A camera and other gear. Eddy applied for more than forty patents when he worked at RCA's experimental television station in New York City during the 1930s and was considered an electrical engineering genius. During World War II he headed the navy's highly selective Electronics Training Program. He later made significant contributions to WBKB, Chicago's first commercial television station. George Cranston was named station manager of WBAP-TV before Channel 5 went on the air.

LEFT
Comedian Milton Berle was television's first major star. As the host of NBC network's *Texaco Star Theater*, he relied on his vaudeville and radio days for inspiration. Visiting guest stars like Ethel Merman (right) helped make his weekly program reach number one in the Nielsen ratings. Berle, who referred to himself as Uncle Miltie, and his program were both honored with Emmys in the second year of the awards. He still holds the title of Mr. Television. Berle's programs were kinescoped, the process networks initally used to share their programs with their affiliates. The shows were filmed off of a master TV screen while the live program was in progress. Copies of the film were then mailed to affiliates for broadcasting, sometimes a week or more later. Live network programming via coaxial cable and microwave relay did not become available until 1952.

The first few months the station presented programs four hours each evening, Wednesday through Saturday. This included both local and network programs. A test pattern with audio tone was shown four hours during the day and four hours at night. Within six months Channel 5 increased programs to seven days a week for a total of thirty-five to forty hours. This was a combination of local and network news and programs. By May 1949 the viewing area had grown from a few hundred TV households to about 9,200. Many store windows displayed working TV sets, and people gathered inside and out to watch what was on TV. The screens were small, just six

to eight inches, but the cabinets were huge. They had to be enormous to accommodate the massive picture tubes.

We didn't get our first TV set at home until the summer of 1949. It was a black-and-white Hoffman with an "Easy-Vision" screen that gave it a greenish tint to cut the glare and make it easier on viewers' eyes. Our Hoffman was a table model with a twelve-inch screen. As best I can recall, it cost between $300 and $400, which was a lot of money in 1949—especially considering Phil's salary was less than one hundred dollars a week, and mine was thirty!

WBAP-TV PROGRAM SCHEDULE
FOR NEWSPAPER CLOCKS

MONDAY, NOVEMBER 21
2:00--TEST PATTERN
4:00--"SPOT THE SLIDE" - Chem Terry in a TV quiz show. Studio.
4:15--"WHAT'S NEW LADIES" - With Wilma Rutherford. Studio.
4:45--"STUMP US" - Musical quiz with Frank Mills. Studio
5:15--"PLAYTIME" - Fun for the youngsters with Mary Parker. Studio.
5:45--"SEE-SAW ZOO" - WBAP-TV's all-original puppet show with Dean
       Raymond. Studio.
6:00--"KUKLA, FRAN AND OLLIE" - TV puppet players. NBC.
6:30--"SHOWROOM" - Radio favorite Morton Downey. N B C.
6:45--"ORGAN MELODIES" - Studio musical with William Barclay.
7:00--"TELE-THEATER" - Margo in "His Name Is Jason". NBC
7:30--"FLYING X RANCHBOYS" - Mel Cox and his musical ranchhands. Studio
8:00--"DAVY CROCKETT'S OPRY HOUSE" - Presenting "Pecos Kids" with
       Fred Kohler, Jr.
9:00--"NEWS FINAL" - Tomorrow morning's headlines. Studio.
9:05--"WEATHER TELE-FACTS" - Tomorrow's weather report. Studio.
9:10--"SPORTS PREVIEWS" - With Bud Watson.
9:25--"ROLLER DERBY" - Direct from Fort Worth's Northside Coliseum.
10:30--SIGN OFF
(All test patterns accompanied by 1000 cycle tone for installations.)

TUESDAY, NOVEMBER 22
2:00--TEST PATTERN
4:00--"HERE'S TO YOUR HEALTH" - A guide to better living. Studio.
4:15--"TCU IN REVIEW" - Studio variety show.
4:45--"STUMP US" - Frank Mills emcees a studio quiz.
5:15--"PLAYTIME" - Fun for the youngsters with Mary Parker. Studio.
5:45--"SEE-SAW ZOO" - WBAP-TV's all-original puppet show. Studio.
6:00--"KUKLA, FRAN AND OLLIE" - TV puppet players. NBC
6:22--"ORGAN MELODIES" - Featuring William Barclay. Studio.
6:30--"SHOWROOM" - Starring songstress Roberta Quinlan. NBC.
6:45--"TEXAS NEWS" - Fort Worth-Dallas area news events.
7:00--"STAR THEATER" - Featuring Milton Berle and guests. NBC
8:00--"THE LIFE OF RILEY" - With Jackie Gleason in the title role. NBC.
8:30--"FASHION REFLECTIONS" - With Nona Lou Greene. Studio.
8:45--"STARRING BORIS KARLOFF" - New ABC mystery series.
9:15--"TOUCHDOWN TIDE" - Highlights of Southwest Conference games
       played Saturday as filmed by WBAP-TV's news room.
9:30--"MELODY SHOP" - Fifteen musical minutes with Betty Brockwell.
9:45--"NEWS FINAL" - Tomorrow morning's headlines. Studio.
9:50--"WEATHER TELE-FACTS" - Tomorrow's weather forecast. Studio.
9:55--SIGN OFF
(All test patterns accompanied by 1000 cycle tone for installations.)

WEDNESDAY, NOVEMBER 23
2:00--TEST PATTERN
4:00--"SPOT THE SLIDES" - Chem Terry in a TV quiz. Studio.
4:15--"WHAT'S NEW LADIES" - With Wilma Rutherford. Studio.
4:45--"STUMP US" - Musical quiz with Frank Mills. Studio.
5:15--"PLAYTIME" - Fun for the youngsters with Mary Parker. Studio.
5:45--"SEE-SAW ZOO" - Studio puppet show with Dean Raymond.
6:00--"KUKLA, FRAN AND OLLIE" - TV puppet players. Studio.
6:30--"SHOWROOM" - With radio favorite Morton Downey. Studio.
6:45--"ORGAN MELODIES" - Studio musical with William Barclay.
7:00--"GARDENING CAN BE FUN" - With Layne Beaty. Studio.
7:20--"FITZPATRICK TRAVELTALK: SCOTLAND" - Featurette.
7:30--"THE CLOCK" - "The Fighter" with William Thurnhurst. NBC.
8:00--"WHAT IS IT?" - TV game of charades. Studio.
8:30--"YOUR SONG AND MINE" - With Durelle Alexander and guests. Studio.
8:45--"HUNGRY MINDS" - The story of today's children of Europe.
9:00--"WHO SAID THAT?" - Quiz with Bob Trout and guests. NBC.
9:30--"NEWS FINAL" - Tomorrow morning's headlines. Studio.
9:35--"WEATHER TELE-FACTS" - Tomorrow's weather reporter. Studio.
9:40--"ROLLER DERBY" - From Northside Coliseum.
10:30--SIGN OFF
(All test patterns accompanied by 1000 cycle tone for installations.)

ABOVE
A few months after signing on, the WBAP-TV broadcast schedule expanded to seven days a week with almost forty hours of programming. In addition to local programs, the station drew from both NBC and ABC network program options, after signing the first dual network affiliation agreement in August 1948. The agreement lasted until 1957, when NBC signed the paperwork to make WBAP-TV their exclusive affiliate in the Fort Worth-Dallas market.

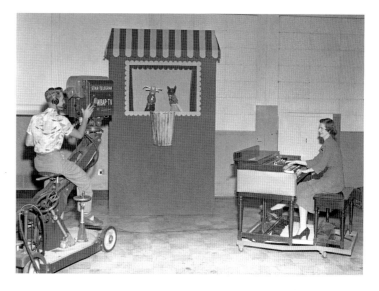

ABOVE
See-Saw Zoo was one of Channel 5's first locally produced programs. Professional puppeteer Dean Raymond wrote, designed, produced, and starred in the daily children's show, with organist Rosemary Lurie providing musical accompaniment.

ABOVE
Maurice the Bum Steer (center) was one of *See-Saw Zoo*'s main characters. An innovative talent, Dean Raymond was a Channel 5 employee who devoted all of his time to the puppet show. Rosemary Lurie split her staff duties between *See-Saw Zoo* and the WBAP film department.

LEFT
Clarabelle (second from left), from the NBC network's hit show *Howdy Doody*, and the future Icky Twerp, a.k.a. Bill Camfield (left) stop by for a visit on Mary Parker's *Playtime* children's show. Clarabelle was in town for a live appearance at Leonard's Department Store, where Camfield worked in the advertising department. In 1954, Camfield joined KFJZ-TV, where he created a series of legendary TV characters, among them Gorgon, host of *Nightmare Theater*, and Ichamore Twerpwhistle, the host of *Slam-Bang Theater*.

The NBC network provided a few hours of programming in the evening. One of the earliest shows was the Tuesday night *Texaco Star Theater*, starring Milton Berle. Uncle Miltie was an enormous hit and the main subject around Wednesday morning water coolers.

Afternoon kiddie shows caught on big time. The network provided *Howdy Doody* and *Kukla, Fran, and Ollie*. Locally we had *See-Saw Zoo*. Dean Raymond was our puppeteer. He also wrote and produced the show. Rosemary Lurie was the organist and music director. Rosemary's husband, Al Lurie, was a member of the production staff.

Playtime was a local live show with Mary Parker reading stories to children on set.

Mary was a curvacious, good-looking blonde who had worked in Hollywood but was back in Fort Worth. She probably had more daddies watching than kiddies, but after a short run Mary Parker left *Playtime*.

This brought a new children's program called *Kitty's Playhouse*, presented by Kitty Adkins. Kitty took the program beyond reading stories to include activities for the children who were on set with her, as well as the ones watching at home. *Kitty's Playhouse* and later *Kitty's Wonderland* were big favorites with both parents and kids. Kitty's husband, Luther Adkins, was in charge of station personnel. He also hosted *Christian Questions*, a weekly panel show with religious leaders discussing various topics.

ABOVE
Kitty's Playhouse was a popular local children's program that starred Kitty Adkins. The program was retooled to become *Kitty's Wonderland*, a phenomenally popular hour-long daily morning show for children from two to six. The program featured story telling, cartoons, contests, birthday announcements, a get-well club, and helpful hints. In 1957, *Kitty's Wonderland* was the highest rated daytime show in the Fort Worth-Dallas market.

ABOVE
In a stark departure from her children's program persona, Mary Parker poses for a travel commercial.

OPPOSITE
Margret McDonald was Channel 5's director of home economics and host of the locally produced *What's Cookin'* show, with Bill Guy (right) as her cohost. She later hosted *Texas Living,* where she presented food, fashions, and interior decorating, with Frank Mills as her cohost. Margret McDonald Rimmer was elected to the Fort Worth City Council in 1971 and became the first female to be named mayor pro tem of Fort Worth.

RIGHT
Each week Nona Lou Greene's *Fashion Reflections* featured live models from different department stores with a live studio audience. Greene (between the two models) was the *Star-Telegram's* fashion writer and regularly traveled to New York to cover the latest fashion trends. Greene's viewers loved her free-form commentary.

Margret McDonald's *What's Cookin'* was a daily program of recipes and homemaking information. The studio had a full operating kitchen. The minute the cameras were off, the crew rushed to gobble up the day's recipes. Margret, who was an engaging personality as well as a good cook, appeared on set with announcer Bill Guy. When color TV arrived in 1954, the show's title changed to *Texas Living,* and Frank Mills joined Margret as cohost.

Nona Lou Greene did a weekly nighttime show, *Fashion Reflections.* Nona Lou was a fashion reporter for the *Star-Telegram.* While live models circled around her, Nona Lou ad-libbed commentary, whatever came to mind. Nona Lou had no filter. Audiences loved her off-the-cuff comments, probably because they were in contrast to the usual sedate fashion commentaries.

Fashions also were a regular part of the *Ann Alden* afternoon program, presented by Stripling's Department Store of Fort Worth. In real life Ann Alden was Ann Pugh, a local actress and writer.

LEFT
Durelle Alexander appeared on a number of early Channel 5 programs. An audience favorite, she was a regularly featured singer on *Saturday Night Barn Dance*. She had been a Hollywood child actress who appeared in silent *Our Gang* comedies and *Hollywood Junior Follies* before becoming a big band singer. She toured with Eddy Duchin and was a featured vocalist on *Paul Whiteman's Musical Varieties* radio show. In 1936, she appeared with Whiteman in Billy Rose's Casa Mañana in Fort Worth, where she met and married Edmund Van Zandt.

The big show was *Saturday Night Barn Dance*. It had everything. Local square dance clubs provided square dancers. Sixteen ladies in bouffant crinoline skirts took up half of the studio, but there still was room for a western band, horses, and guest stars. It was a big deal and sold more than a few TV sets.

The daytime hit was *The Bobby Peters Show*. "Voot," as he liked to be called, was a showman who fronted a band that played nightclubs. His nightclub act was an evening of dance music that included a show with costumes and skits. Bobby was a cool dude with stunning salt and pepper hair—very hip. So the station hired him to do a weekday afternoon variety show. Bobby pantomimed records, did skits, told jokes, and goofed around with the crew for an hour each day.

His favorite thing to do was to yell, just before airtime, "Hey guys I need you for ten minutes." He'd hand out props and wigs and costumes and say, "When I do this, you do that. Watch me and you'll know what to say." Being the largest guy on the crew, Phil Wygant always got the female roles. Once disguised with wig and costume, Phil turned into a five-star ham. Bobby loved it. As time went on pianist Jimmy Livingston and singer Lettie Reynolds joined the show. I don't know how he did it, but Bobby Peters put on an hour-long show every day with no producer, no writers, no costumer, no prop person, and no production budget. He did it all! Today a show like that needs two minutes of credits to name the staff.

OPPOSITE
By far, Channel 5's most popular evening program was *Saturday Night Barn Dance*, featuring live musical performances and dancing by local square dance clubs like the Square D Club, Circle 8, and Roundup. Musician Ken "Cowboy Ken" Houghins was the host of the show, with Calvin Moore doing the square dance calling. Horses added atmosphere.

ABOVE
The Bobby Peters Show was WBAP's runaway daytime hit. A born showman of boundless talent and energy, Bobby became an instant Channel 5 star. He was also on WBAP radio.

ABOVE CENTER
By day, Peters worked at WBAP; by night, he was a well-known entertainer and band leader who performed regularly at area nightclubs.

ABOVE FAR RIGHT
Growing up on the East Coast, Peters started in show business when he was still a teenager. In the 1930s, he was a regular on Pittsburgh radio and later formed a touring orchestra. He came to Fort Worth in 1939 and briefly opened his own nightclub on East Belknap.

ABOVE
Peters's novel fairy tale reenactments delighted children and their parents, too.

ABOVE
Five days a week Peters almost single-handedly filled up an hour-long show with an endless series of hilarious personas. Regarded as the ultimate hipster, Peters often spoke in beatnik slang.

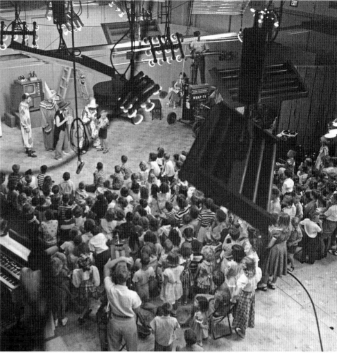

ABOVE
Pandemonium frequently broke out in the audience when Bobby handed out freebies to the kids.

ABOVE FAR RIGHT
The main Channel 5 studio could seat as many as 150 audience members in folding chairs at the rear of the space. Bobby's kid shows could accommodate even larger audiences by seating children on the floor up front, near the action.

ABOVE
Pianist Jimmy Livingston was a regular on Bobby Peters's shows. Livingston was also on *Texas Living*, where he demonstrated do-it-yourself handyman ideas.

ABOVE
Bobby Peters (in top hat) frequently recruited the production crew to perform in his last-minute ad-libbed skits. Being the largest in the crew, Phil Wygant (left) often got the female roles.

LEFT
Two weeks after Channel 5 signed on in 1948, four of the biggest elephants from Ringling Brothers and Barnum and Bailey Circus made a muddy entrance into the yet-to-be-completed studio building. Program Director Bob Gould described their promotional appearance to *Telescene* magazine: "It hadn't rained for two or three months, but the day the elephants came, it poured. It was pretty wet inside, too; those elephants brought in a lot of water through their kidneys."

LEFT
Elephant trainer Hugo Schmitt directed the animals on the Channel 5 set to do headstands, ride piggy-back, and flip his wife, Charlotte, high into the air. It was the first time a circus act was televised inside a TV studio.

ABOVE
While he was still a student at North Texas State College, Pat Boone made his TV debut on WBAP as the youthful host of *Teen Time*, sponsored by Foremost Dairy. After winning on the influential national TV show *Arthur Godfrey's Talent Scouts*, Boone became a national singing sensation. His clean-cut, All-American persona was the antithesis of Elvis Presley, who shared the top of the charts with Boone. By 1957, Boone was the host of his own TV variety show on ABC, *The Pat Boone Chevy Showroom*.

ABOVE
Visual comedy was a common fallback on many of the early programs.

ABOVE
When the Shrine Circus came to town, animal acts were often booked on one of the locally produced Channel 5 programs—here, on *The Ann Alden Show*. Ann Alden is on the left.

When network afternoon programs replaced him, Bobby moved to Saturday mornings for *The Bobby Peters Jamboree*. Kids loved him. When Bobby drove his red Oldsmobile convertible with the top down, kids lined the sidewalks shouting and waving at him. Voot said, "It's hard to take bows when you're driving!"

I learned a lot from Bobby Peters about being yourself on television. The camera is a magnifying glass and an X-ray. You can't fool the camera. You might get by putting on an act for a while, but sooner or later the camera will "out" you. It's best to be yourself, and if you're having a bad day, you hope the audience will accept you as one of them.

In 1953 Pat Boone made his television debut on WBAP-TV. The show *Teenage Downbeat* featured Pat behind a soda fountain in white cap and apron. Local teenagers performed, and Pat sang. He always projected the all-American-boy image. The big sweat with Pat was worrying if he'd show up on time. Pat was married and a student at North Texas State University in Denton, now called the University of North Texas. His wife Shirley was the daughter of country music star Red Foley. It was a forty-five-minute drive from Denton to the Fort Worth studio, but the question was always whether Pat would have enough gas and would his old car make it without breaking down.

ABOVE
The WBAP production crew was responsible for all aspects of production, from designing and building sets to lighting and sometimes even directing. (Left to right) Bob Grammer, David Timmons, Phil Wygant, Ed Milner, Sid Smith, Richard Bice.

ABOVE RIGHT
Besides her singing appearances, Durelle Alexander also did cooking demonstrations and crafts.

RIGHT
Cowboy Ken Houghins (back row, right) had a nightly WBAP radio program in addition to hosting the weekly *Saturday Night Barn Dance*, which was called *Hoffman Hayloft* during the years Hoffman Television sponsored the show. The family variety show included special segments to appeal to the younger generation.

RIGHT
Advertisers used the Channel 5 studios and crew to film commercials and promotional segments for their products, such as Motorola's *Dinner Date with Dottie* which booked live musicians to demonstrate Motorola products.

ABOVE
Stump Us was one of Channel 5's earliest musical quiz shows, hosted by Frank Mills and costarring staff organist Bill Barclay. Viewers called in to request a song for Barclay to play, and if Barclay didn't know it, the caller got a prize. I served as the program's assistant, taking the phone calls and showing off the prizes.

Even in the early fifties we all knew Pat Boone would be a big star. He went from Texas to New York, and after winning on *Arthur Godfrey's Talent Scouts* television show, Pat was on his way to stardom.

New local shows were starting every week. Anyone with an idea for a live show was free to toss it in the ring. When the continuity department moved its office to the TV studio, I started doing on-camera work. I kept my hair and makeup camera-ready so that I could go from office to studio on short notice for an on-camera appearance.

I was considered too young to host a show, so I was always the assistant. I was Vanna White before there was a Vanna White. In one program called *Stump Us*, viewers would call in to request a song. I took the call, gave the information to emcee Frank Mills, and he'd ask staff organist Bill Barclay to play it.

ABOVE

The Budweiser Clydesdale horse team was one of the most popular acts at the Fort Worth Fat Stock Show and Rodeo, appearing there every year. The team never missed the chance to stop by the Channel 5 studios.

RIGHT
An iconic St. Louis tradition, the
Clydesdales were included in President
Harry Truman's 1949 inaugural parade.

ABOVE
Anyone with an idea for a
new TV show was encouraged
to present it. Many local
productions quickly
came and went.

ABOVE
The Ann Alden Show was an afternoon program sponsored by Stripling's Department
Store, starring local actress Ann Barham Pugh. She graduated from Paschal and TCU
and later attended the University of Southern California and the Pasadena Playhouse
Theatre School. After being screen-tested by Metro-Goldwyn-Mayer in Hollywood, she
moved to New York where she worked in off-Broadway and summer stock. In later
years, she wrote several musical theater plays.

RIGHT

Channel 5 public affairs programs were occasionally able to book well-known political figures, like Speaker of the US House of Representatives Sam Rayburn. A Bonham, Texas, native, Rayburn was one of the most powerful politicians of his time, but preferred staying out of the limelight. Known for his high standards of integrity, he was a member of the House for forty-eight years and served as Speaker for a record seventeen years. A Democrat representing Texas District 4, Rayburn worked with Lyndon B. Johnson's father, Sam, when they were both in the Texas legislature, and Rayburn later mentored Lyndon B. Johnson in his rise to power.

RIGHT

Another Channel 5 public affairs programming coup was the special appearance of Bishop Fulton Sheen. Sheen was the host of the unlikely hit network television program *Life is Worth Living*, which debuted in 1951. Every week Sheen lectured extemporaneously in front of a camera and live audience. The straightforward, simply staged show won two Emmys and landed Sheen on the cover of *Time* in 1952. Actor Martin Sheen so admired Bishop Sheen that he chose "Sheen" when he changed his name from Ramon Gerard Antonio Estevez.

ABOVE

Teenage Downbeat was Channel 5's local version of Dick Clark's national hit show *American Bandstand*. Using the Bandstand record-hop format, host Tom Mullarkey (left) interviewed big name guest stars like Frankie Laine (right), who came through town to promote their latest records. Laine enjoyed a long and enduring recording career as a jazz and pop singer starting in the 1930s. In the 1950s, he hosted three of his own television variety shows. Today, he is best remembered for singing the theme song on the TV show *Rawhide*.

ABOVE

Host Tom Mullarkey (right) was a seasoned on-air talent who had been an announcer and writer for KLIF radio before joining WBAP-TV as a sports announcer and the host of *Teenage Downbeat*. He knew how to connect with the teen audience.

ABOVE

The weekday teen show eventually moved to Saturdays and expanded to include contest giveaways and pre-teens, too.

ABOVE

Unexpected guests occasionally showed up on *Teenage DownBeat*, such as when the *Queen for a Day* Cadillac drove in for a visit. *Queen for a Day* was a popular NBC show in which female contestants suffering various personal plights told their stories to host Jack Bailey, and a studio audience judged which of them had the most compelling story. An applause meter determined who would be crowned "Queen for a Day" and receive a bounty of prizes.

RIGHT

Staff celebrations, led by Margret McDonald and Bill Guy (front and center), called for balloons and refreshments. I'm at the very end of the food line behind them (at right). In front of me, from right to left, are my boss, Program Director Bob Gould; Chief Engineer Super Stinson; Ruby Hankins; and Bessie Coldiron (in the dark suit). Besides working in the continuity department, I was often enlisted to be the on-camera assistant for various local programs.

RIGHT

Johnny Hay (left) joined Channel 5 in 1949. He was involved in all capacities of programming and was also a skillful caricaturist. He directed programs and was the host of several, including *The Johnny Hay Show*, an interview show where he drew a caricature of each day's guest before introducing them on the set. One of his most famous guests was the legendary film director and producer, Alfred Hitchcock (second from right) who was promoting his latest film, *I Confess*. Hitchcock was also a talented caricaturist, so after admiring Hay's rendition of him, Hitch drew his own self-portrait and signed it. *I Confess* stars Anne Baxter (second from left) and Roger Dann (right) signed it, too. A few years later Hitchcock became known for the simple line-drawing caricature of himself in the title sequence of his long-running TV show *Alfred Hitchcock Presents*.

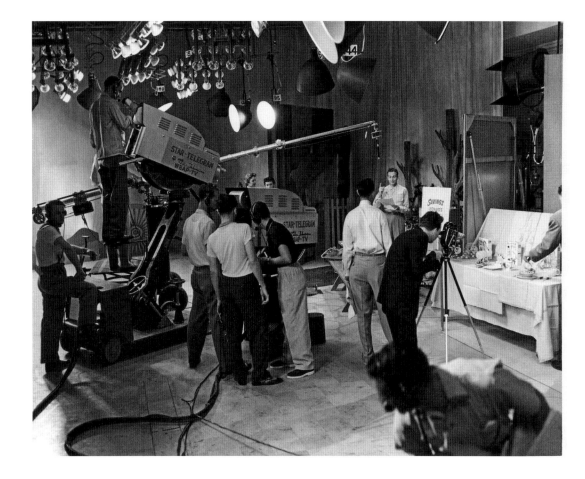

LEFT
Commercials were read live on the air. In this photograph, Frank Mills presents a Leonard's Department Store commercial in between *Texas Living* segments.

If Barclay didn't know it, the caller would get a prize. The prize might be a box of stationery or a toiletry set or a box of candy. Some callers would protest that Barclay wasn't playing the right thing. Bill would never admit he didn't know the song. He'd rip off a few chords and claim that was it. Then Frank Mills would have to decide who was right.

Frank Mills was an institution. He came to Fort Worth in 1936 from Iowa, on his way to Hollywood with his friend Ronald Reagan, who was known as "Dutch" back in Iowa. Mills heard that WBAP radio had announcer openings. He auditioned and was hired. Mills stayed in Texas. "Dutch" went on to Hollywood.

Years later, before he ran for governor of California, Reagan came to the WBAP-TV studios for an appearance. He passed Mills in the hall and said, "Hi, Frank," and as Reagan kept walking Frank replied, "Hi, Dutch." End of greeting. Reagan left the building. It was the first and last time they had seen one another since 1936, and they wouldn't see each other again. Frank would laugh when telling that story.

ABOVE
Even though I had no serious aspirations to become an actress, my husband Phil and I became founding members of the Fort Worth Community Theater. I acted in several plays with the theater, including *Oh Men! Oh Women!*, here with my friend Katherine "Kiki" Smith.

ABOVE
Frank Mills was the cohost of the interview show *Texas Living* with Margret McDonald. Because of his many years of announcing on WBAP radio, Mills exuded an amiable air of confidence that put his interview subjects at ease.

LEFT
Moonlighting from their American Airlines jobs, (left to right) meteorologists Harold Taft, Walter Porter, and Bob Denney based the *Weather Telefacts* format on weather briefing techniques used by military pilots. The program was scheduled after the *Texas News* every night and generally ran for about five minutes, but could run longer, depending on the weather. Occasionally, short twenty-second-long current condition updates that showed the weather dials were inserted before or after commercials.

ABOVE RIGHT
After Harold Taft was named WBAP's chief meteorologist, his no-nonsense broadcast style gained him many loyal viewers. A graduate of Phillips University, he was in the Army Air Corps during World War II and attended Army Weather School.

Mills was a natural for television. He had the looks, the personality, and the voice. He was one of those guys "Hired Hand" announcer Harold Hough had in mind when he said they had "lace on their tonsils." Were it not for Frank Mills, neither Phil nor I would have been in Texas because he hired Phil for staff announcer in 1947.

From its debut on October 31, 1949, *Weather Telefacts* set the standard for WBAP-TV'S weather forecasting. Three meteorologists from American Airlines formed the staff. Harold Taft, Bob Denney, and Walter Porter rotated the nightly programs with Harold Taft as chief. Taft, who became known as the "Dean of TV Meteorologists," was the first meteorologist west of the Mississippi to give weathercasts on TV. He wrote the bible on TV weather forecasting. In the early days, they drew the maps and data with colored chalk on large paper sheets. You could always tell the meteorologists by the green chalk dust under their nails.

The *Texas News* was the station's signature. I can still hear in my head the Texas Electric Service Company theme song while the animated Reddy Kilowatt figure showed everything electricity did for everyday living. TESCO was a longtime sponsor of the newscast. By 1949, the *Texas News* was named the nation's best news program by the Radio/TV News Directors Association. WBAP-TV News Director James A. Byron and his staff repeated that win six more times. This was a forerunner of many prestigious awards to come, including four Edward R. Murrow Awards in 2017 for the nation's best newscast and overall station excellence, making Dallas-Fort Worth NBC 5 the most awarded TV station in the country that year. In 2018, the KXAS-TV investigative team won a coveted Peabody Award, giving the station its first-ever Peabody.

ABOVE

Channel 5's opening night program included a ten-minute *Texas News* segment with a live voice-over. It was the first TV news broadcast in the Southwest. *Texas News* crews followed news events like the landmark Fort Worth flood of May 17, 1949. Floodwaters can be seen in the background at left.

LEFT

In 1959, WBAP installed a rooftop weather radar station. WBAP radio's Bill Mack dubbed Taft (shown here) "The World's Greatest Weatherman."

ABOVE
The award-winning *Texas News* was the brainchild of WBAP News Director James A. Byron. A veteran newspaper man, he was appointed news director of WBAP radio in 1944. Byron's duties were expanded to include WBAP-TV while it was still in development. A highly respected journalist, he was instrumental in making the *Texas News* one of the station's signature programs.

ABOVE LEFT
The *Texas News* film reels were put together by the WBAP newsroom staff, which included (seated left to right) Lillard Hill, who read the live voiceovers, and Doyle Vinson, who ran the department under the direction of James Byron. (Standing left to right) photographer Jimmie Mundell; reporter James Kerr, who ran the Dallas news bureau; Lynn Trammell, who was head of the film department. Trammell also had a Sunday night poetry program on WBAP radio.

ABOVE
All of the *Texas News* film footage shot in the field was processed immediately at the station's on-site film laboratory and sent to the film editors who cut and arranged the raw film into a visual story. Afterwards, a script was written to fit the pictures.

ABOVE
The main studio lighting was housed in thirty-one banks of lights that were suspended from the ceiling by a pipe framework. The lights were normally in a fixed grid pattern but could be rotated by means of rope controls grouped on a lighting bridge that was accessed by a catwalk running along both sides of the studio.

ABOVE
RCA Board Chairman David Sarnoff (left) and Amon G. Carter flipped a switch at 3:00 p.m. on May 15, 1954, making all WBAP-TV broadcasts in color from that day forward. At that time, only 125 color TV sets were estimated to be within the broadcast area.

ABOVE RIGHT
May 15, 1954, marked the first live color telecast in Texas. Harold Hough (right) hosted NBC network bigwigs, including Harry Bannister, NBC vice president (left), for "Color Day," a three-hour live extravaganza utilizing the station's three brand-new color cameras. The cameras were delivered less than a week before the big day, but the cables were missing and didn't get to Fort Worth until twenty hours before show time. NBC officials warned production director Bob Gould that the color cameras would get too hot to last for three hours straight.

ABOVE
Amon G. Carter (center) presented Shady Oak hats to David Sarnoff, RCA Board Chairman (left), and Robert Sarnoff, executive vice president of NBC (right), who came to Fort Worth to participate in WBAP's "Color Day."

ABOVE
From the control room above the studios director Jimmy Turner (left) called the camera shots to the switching engineer.

ABOVE
To accommodate the new color cameras, all the studio lighting had to be replaced before Color Day. Prior to ordering the new equipment, Phil Wygant spent two weeks in New York observing the lighting challenges NBC network encountered with their color broadcasts.

On May 15, 1954, WBAP-TV turned from black and white to "living color." When the NBC suits heard that the station was planning a three-hour live program to introduce its color programming, they immediately dispatched two vice presidents from New York to tell the local kids that it was impossible to do a three-hour live program because the color cameras would not hold up that long. They would go to black. Apparently it was too late to make changes. We locals proceeded with our living color extravaganza.

The show had everything but dancing elephants. They would have been turned down. Not colorful enough. The show featured square dancers, a western band, singing groups, tap dancers, magicians, all in colorful array. Reilly Nail was in charge of putting the show together. Reilly had produced shows while a student at Princeton.

ABOVE
Nothing demonstrated WBAP's new color capability
better than *Saturday Night Barn Dance.*

ABOVE
The ever-gracious Margret McDonald interviewed
an American Indian chief on the colorcast of *Texas Living*.

ABOVE RIGHT
Teenage DownBeat staged a formal studio prom
for the new color cameras.

RIGHT
Fort Worth Zoo's Pete the Python was a featured guest at Channel 5's
seventh anniversary celebration. Pete became a *cause célèbre* after
he escaped from his cage at the zoo and went missing for two weeks.
The eighteen-foot-long snake was discovered near the zoo's office,
and after a brief struggle was returned back to his cage.

RIGHT
WBAP's new 1,113-foot transmission tower was designed to increase the station's signal coverage from 6,000 square miles to over 17,000 square miles.

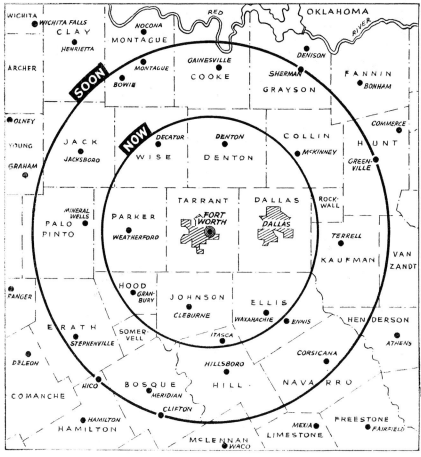

My job that day was assistant to the director Sid Smith. I had the script, what there was of it, and the rundown. The NBC suits were in and out of the control room. The first two hours were smooth. About halfway into the third hour, camera three went out. Sid took camera two, but was worried about getting a camera to the next act at the end of the studio. The audio man Warren Ritchie spoke up and said, "At the end of this number have camera two zoom in, lose focus, do a fast pan to the end of the studio. Then come back to focus."

They did, and we made it through the rest of the three-hour show with two cameras. The NBC suits were speechless. I wish I could have heard what they told their bosses back in New York about the crazy Texans.

The three-hour special probably was seen on a handful of color sets, most of which were in store windows, but from that day forward WBAP-TV broadcast all of its local programs in color. In 1954 WBAP-TV televised more hours of color programs per week than NBC.

OPPOSITE
When WBAP's new tower went into operation in September 1954, the farthest point to report good reception was 296 miles away from Fort Worth. By March 1957, fifty-three Texas and Oklahoma counties were able to tune in to Channel 5.

FOUR

My First Television Show

Amon G. Carter died in 1955, just a few months after flipping on the switch for Channel 5 to go all-color. His son, Amon G. Carter Jr., took over the family-owned media conglomerate, one of the largest privately held publishing and broadcasting empires in Texas.

OPPOSITE

After twelve years of running the Channel 5 continuity department and filling in as an on-camera assistant, I finally got my chance to start doing on-camera interviews.

Harold Hough remained vice president and director of the broadcast division of Carter Communications, as well as circulation manager of the *Star-Telegram* newspaper. Mr. Hough had two offices, one at the *Star-Telegram* and one at Channel 5. He spent most of his time at the paper downtown, coming to WBAP about once a week. Station Manager George Cranston was in charge of the day-to-day operations of Channel 5.

In 1960 Mr. Hough decided the station needed more local programs on topics that were colorful, like ladies' clothing. The program people came up with a daily show they called *Dateline* (not to be confused with NBC network's *Dateline* that debuted thirty years later). Channel 5's *Dateline* had a segment featuring live models in colorful attire. Each week a local store presented the fashions and models. There was a script that Lynn Trammell read off-camera during her lunch hour. Lynn was head of the film department, overseeing the many programs broadcast on film. Lynn had one of those voices you love to listen to. She did a radio show on Sunday nights reading poetry.

ABOVE

Lynn Trammell (right) hosted *Dateline* during her lunch breaks. She interviewed celebrities like veteran actor Frank McHugh (left), who was starring in *Mister Roberts* at Casa Mañana in 1960. Show announcer Larry Morrell (center) helped to warm everyone up before the interviews.

ABOVE LEFT

Amon G. Carter Jr. (left) took over running Carter Publications after his father died in 1955. Harold Hough (right) stayed on as vice president and director of Carter Publications' broadcast division, as well as circulation manager of the *Star-Telegram*. A few years later, Hough was named Dean of American Broadcasters by the National Association of Broadcasters.

LEFT

Lynn Trammell (right) and announcer Larry Morrell (center) talk to actor Jack Carson (left) about his starring role in *Make a Million* at Casa Mañana. Carson was active in episodic television in the 1960s, following a successful radio and film career. One of his most memorable film roles was as Wally Fay in *Mildred Pierce*, with Joan Crawford.

RIGHT
Casa Mañana, built in 1958, presented in-the-round New York productions of Broadway musicals. The shows at Casa provided Channel 5 with more opportunities to interview visiting celebrities. The theater's striking silver geodesic dome was designed and developed by Kaiser Aluminum Corporation. Architect A. George King and Associates designed the building. The new theater was sited near the original Casa Mañana, which was built in 1936 for Fort Worth's Frontier Centennial but was demolished in 1942.

RIGHT
Before her appearance on *Dateline*, famous burlesque fan dancer Sally Rand (center), star of "Sally Rand's Nude Ranch" at the 1936 Frontier Centennial, visited with *Dateline* director Sid Smith (left) and floor manager Ed Milner.

ABOVE

Program director Bob Gould asked me to fill in as host for that day's *Dateline* when Lynn Trammell called in sick.

ABOVE LEFT

Larry Morrell greeted comedian Joe E. Brown before his *Dateline* interview to promote his appearance in Casa's *Father of the Bride* in 1961. Brown started his entertainment career in films beginning in 1928 and continuing through the 1960s, with a featured role in *Some Like It Hot* and cameos in *Around the World in 80 Days* and *It's A Mad, Mad, Mad, Mad World.*

LEFT

Dateline host Lynn Trammell interviewed actress Laraine Day (left) when she was in Fort Worth to star in *The Women* at Casa Mañana. Day was best known for playing the girlfriend in the seven-picture Dr. Kildare series starring actor Lew Ayres in the 1930s and 1940s.

RIGHT
Lynn Trammell had always been a reluctant *Dateline* host, preferring instead to run the Channel 5 film department. After I did well as her substitute, Lynn encouraged Bob Gould to ask me to take over the show permanently.

Dateline began to get an audience, so they started adding interviews. Next thing Lynn was hosting the show on camera during her lunch hour. One Monday morning I was at my desk writing copy when Bob Gould, the program director, came in and said, "Lynn has called in sick so you'll have to do *Dateline* today." It was 11 a.m. The show went on at noon. He said, "Talk to Sid Smith. He's directing and he'll tell you what to do."

I did a quick makeup and hair check and headed to the studio. Sid said, "I'm not sure what's on so let's see who shows up." Fortunately, Larry Morrell was the announcer on the show, so I had someone for backup. I don't remember what or who was on besides the fashion segment, but we got through it okay. The only complaints from viewers who phoned in were, "Can't you put Bobbie on a cushion? We can't see her behind that desk." The next day and from then on I sat on two Yellow Pages phone books.

Lynn had the flu, so she was out the rest of the week, but before she returned she called in and said, "Bobbie is a natural for the show. Why don't you get her to do it so I can go back to running my film department?" So in the fall of 1960 I started hosting *Dateline*. I also found myself doing some of the producer duties because the director, Sid Smith, left at 1 p.m. and was not available to book guests. Soon I was named producer and hostess of the show. Little did I know I would be doing that for the next fifteen years.

Photographer Lee Angle was commissioned by Channel 5 to take these portraits of me when I was named the permanent *Dateline* hostess.

LEFT
As the new *Dateline* host, I also took over booking the guests, a task that required doing research and fielding calls. I soon added producer to my job title. I had a full plate because I was still running the continuity department with no support staff.

OPPOSITE
Dateline was the only daily half-hour general interest program in the Dallas-Fort Worth market, and the first in the Southwest to be hosted by a woman. Guests came from all walks of life, from Hollywood celebrities to local chefs, artists, and clergy. My credo became "If it isn't illegal or immoral, I'll put it on."

Dateline was the only show of its kind in the Dallas-Fort Worth market. It was the first daily general-interest TV show in the Southwest and the first daily general-interest show hosted by a woman. Our guest list included astronauts, submarine commanders, circus performers, lions, elephants, Budweiser horses, doctors, politicians, clergy, chefs, artists, and men, women, and children from nearly every community organization in the area. Stars and celebrities were regular fare. Van Cliburn played the piano. Tony Bennett lip-synced "I Left My Heart in San Francisco." Lucille Ball, Ella Fitzgerald, John Wayne, and many more celebrities came for interviews. PR firms in New York and Los Angeles bombarded us with requests to feature their representatives with new products.

FAR LEFT
Film legend Dick Powell (right) was one of my first interviews outside of the Channel 5 studios. I arrived at the Dallas Holiday Inn on North Central Expressway with my husband Phil (left) who was Channel 5's promotion director. Powell was promoting *The Dick Powell Show*, a weekly anthology series that featured the work of such emerging Hollywood talents as Blake Edwards and Aaron Spelling. Powell was known for his work in musical comedies in the 1930s and 1940s and for playing Philip Marlowe in *Murder, My Sweet*.

ABOVE LEFT
As Pat O'Brien's long film career began to wind down, he developed a one-man act that he performed on the stage and in nightclubs throughout the US. Both a leading man and character actor, he was in more than one hundred films, notably *The Front Page*, *Knute Rockne, All American*, *Angels with Dirty Faces*, and *Some Like It Hot*. In 1961, O'Brien starred in the TV sitcom *Harrigan and Son*.

ABOVE
When singer and actress Florence Henderson came on *Dateline* in 1961, she was still a few years away from her career-defining role as Carol Brady on TV's *The Brady Bunch*. Henderson was in Dallas to star in *The Sound of Music* at the State Fair Music Hall.

ABOVE
The setup for the Dick Powell interview inside the Holiday Inn was bare bones: one photographer, one light, one microphone, no sound man, and a 16mm film camera.

RIGHT
While appearing at the Dallas Statler Hilton, country singer Molly Bee came to the Channel 5 studios for an interview. When she was thirteen, Bee signed with Capitol Records and recorded her first hit record with "I Saw Mommy Kissing Santa Claus" in 1952. Pinky Lee cast her to play his sidekick on his nationally televised children's program, *The Pinky Lee Show.*

FAR RIGHT
Plainview, Texas, native Jimmy Dean stopped by *Dateline* to promote his million-selling hit record "Big Bad John," which won him a Grammy in 1962. Dean's self-titled TV variety show went on the air in 1963 and put the spotlight on country music talents such as George Jones, Buck Owens, and Roger Miller, and also gave Muppeteer Jim Henson his first prime-time television exposure.

RIGHT
Legendary song and dance man Donald O'Connor dropped by the Channel 5 studios during his 1964 run at the Dallas Summer Musical's *Little Me.* The son of vaudeville entertainers, O'Connor appeared in more than fifty films, most notably 1952's *Singin' in the Rain.* In the 1940s and 50s, he starred in a series of surprise hit films with Francis, the Talking Mule.

ABOVE
Richard Chamberlain shot to stardom as a young intern in the top ten TV medical drama *Dr. Kildare.* Shortly after the Kildare TV series began, NBC sent Chamberlain on his first media tour, with Fort Worth the first stop. After my interview at Channel 5, we went to a health fair appearance at Will Rogers Memorial Coliseum. Chamberlain was astonished at the throngs of enthusiastic fans who showed up there. Phil Wygant, promotion director for Channel 5, was glad he followed a hunch to hire extra security. Chamberlain later won more hearts with his role in the TV miniseries *The Thorn Birds.*

LEFT
Jane Fonda was at the beginning of her film career when she appeared on *Dateline* in 1964. She made her screen debut in *Tall Story* in 1960, followed by *Walk on the Wild Side* and *Period of Adjustment*. In 1962 she won a Golden Globe award, the first of seven in her career. Still ahead for her were more than fifty films, two Academy Awards, several TV series, decades of political activism, and a side career as a fitness expert.

LEFT
The Beverly Hillbillies, (left to right) Donna Douglas, Max Baer Jr., and Irene Ryan were the Clampitt family (minus patriarch Buddy Ebsen). They took TV by storm when their show premiered in 1962. TV viewers kept the program in the top twenty for all but one of the nine seasons of its run.

OPPOSITE
A comedy giant, Jerry Lewis couldn't resist hamming it up during his 1963 interview with Bobbie. It had been a banner year for Lewis with the release of *The Nutty Professor,* which he directed, cowrote, and starred in with Stella Stevens, plus his cameo in *It's A Mad, Mad, Mad, Mad World* and a starring role in *Who's Minding the Store?* Lewis already had two stars on Hollywood Boulevard, one for film and one for television. With singer Dean Martin, Lewis worked in nightclubs, theaters, and radio. Martin and Lewis were in almost twenty films together and were rotating hosts on NBC's *Colgate Comedy Hour*. After the duo split in 1956, Lewis started his solo career with the film *The Delicate Delinquent,* followed by *The Sad Sack, The Bellboy, The Ladies Man,* and *The Errand Boy*. Lewis's commitment to the Muscular Dystrophy Association started in 1952 and grew into the annual twenty-four-hour live *Jerry Lewis MDA Labor Day Telethon*. For sixteen years, I was one of its local emcees.

ABOVE

It was no surprise that Doug McClure landed the recurring role of Trampas in *The Virginian* in 1963. As a youth, McClure developed into a skilled horseman after spending a summer on a cattle ranch and riding rodeo.

ABOVE

When Chuck Connors (left) came on *Dateline*, he brought his new wife Kamala Devi (right) who had just costarred with him in the motion picture *Geronimo*. Connors was cast in many TV roles, the biggest of which was Lucas McCain in *The Rifleman,* which ran from 1958 until 1963. He turned to acting after pursuing a serious career in professional baseball and basketball. His first film role was in *Pat and Mike* with Spencer Tracy and Katharine Hepburn, and he later starred in Walt Disney's heart-tugging *Old Yeller.* Johnny Hay (second from right) directed many of Bobbie's *Dateline* programs. Sometimes his job involved doing a little on-set housekeeping before show time.

LEFT

Adult Westerns became a television staple starting in 1955 with *The Life and Legend of Wyatt Earp* and *Gunsmoke.* In 1959, there were almost thirty prime-time western series on television. James Drury started his TV career in *Gunsmoke* and also appeared in episodes of *The Rifleman, Rawhide, Cheyenne,* and *Wagon Train.* His biggest part was the title role in *The Virginian,* a role that lasted for 249 episodes over nine years. Drury played the foreman of the Shiloh Ranch. Throughout the run of the series, his character's name was never divulged; he was simply called The Virginian.

RIGHT
Singer and teen idol Frankie Avalon starred with Annette Funicello in a series of beach party films. When he stopped by Channel 5, he was promoting *Beach Blanket Bingo*, the best known of their beach films. Starting in 1959, Avalon had a successful career as a singer. "Venus" was his first recording to chart, staying at number one on the Billboard charts for five weeks. He had more than thirty Billboard-charting singles. He was cast in dramatic roles on episodic TV and in films, including in *The Alamo, Voyage to the Bottom of the Sea,* and *Ski Party.*

ABOVE FAR RIGHT
Following five years as one of the most popular Mouseketeers on Walt Disney's original *Mickey Mouse Club,* Annette Funicello was cast in several Disney-produced television shows and films, including *The Shaggy Dog* and *Babes in Toyland.* She enjoyed a brief career as a pop singer and starred in a series of seven beach genre films, starting with 1963's box office hit *Beach Party,* which she was promoting when she came on *Dateline.*

ABOVE
Gary Clarke played Steve Hill in *The Virginian*, alongside James Drury and Doug McClure.

ABOVE
When I interviewed Dean Jones, he was the star of the new TV series *Ensign O'Toole.* Jones had already enjoyed success with film roles in *Jailhouse Rock* with Elvis Presley, followed by *Imitation General* with Glenn Ford, and *Never So Few* with Frank Sinatra. In 1963, he costarred with Jack Lemmon and Carol Lynley in the film version of *Under the Yum Yum Tree,* but is best remembered for his Disney film roles in *That Darn Cat!* and *The Love Bug* series.

ABOVE

By the time Pat Boone stopped by visit me and the rest of his Channel 5 TV parents in 1963, he had hosted his own network variety show, starred in nine motion pictures, and released more than twenty-five record albums with six number-one hits. The former host of Channel 5's *Teen Time* had come a long way.

ABOVE RIGHT

Vocalist Patti Page was one of the most successful recording artists of the 1950s, beginning with the release of her first platinum-selling recording "With My Eyes Wide Open." In 1951, her "Tennessee Waltz" hit number one on the record charts and stayed there for more than six months. More hit singles quickly followed, including "All My Love (Bolero)," "I Went to Your Wedding," and "(How Much Is That) Doggie in the Window." She was the host of three network television series, *The Patti Page Show* in the summer of 1956, *The Big Record* in 1957, and *The Patti Page Oldsmobile Show* in 1958. Page made film appearances in *Elmer Gantry, Dondi,* and *Boys' Night Out.*

RIGHT

Sing Along With Mitch featured Mitch Miller leading a male chorus in traditional American songs while the lyrics were displayed simultaneously at the bottom of the TV screen. The TV show ran from 1961 until 1964 and resulted in the release of several *Sing Along with Mitch* record albums, including the now-classic Christmas recordings that remain family traditions for many. As head of the Artist and Repertoire for Columbia and Mercury Records, Mitch Miller left his mark on American pop music. He was vocal about his dislike of rock and roll, preferring to add heavy string arrangements and other embellishments to his recordings. Despite his being thought of as a hack schmaltzmeister by some, Miller's track record for producing hits proved his formula worked, at least until the Beatles arrived.

A classically trained concert pianist, Victor Borge turned his legitimate concert career into a one-man comedy act that he brought to Dallas in 1964 for Neiman Marcus's Fortnight salute to Denmark. Borge immigrated to the States in 1940 after the Nazis occupied his native Denmark, and he was soon booked on American radio shows, including Bing Crosby's *Kraft Music Hall*. By 1946, Borge had his own radio show where he developed comedy routines that sustained him through the rest of his career. He appeared on Ed Sullivan's early TV show *Toast of the Town* and frequently performed with symphony orchestras, including the New York Philharmonic, Chicago Symphony Orchestra, and the London Philharmonic.

We usually had four to five segments in our thirty-minute show. Some days it got a little crazy. I remember one show in particular when we had the Texas Boys Choir at one end of the studio, a baby elephant from the Shrine Circus on an interview set, the fashion segment with live models, a doctor talking about immunizations for school children, and another set for a Pam commercial which I did live with no teleprompter. I did it from memory in a casual manner. I knew the product, so it was not difficult. What was difficult that day was that I did the Shrine Circus interview with the baby elephant standing on my foot.

While some stars were repeat guests and would remember me from a previous interview, I never expected to become their new best friend. It was always a professional relationship with one exception—Bob Hope. Bob was a frequent visitor to Dallas-Fort Worth and to Texas. Almost every time he came, we did an interview.

Bandleader Skitch Henderson dropped by *Dateline* before the Fort Worth Symphony Pops concert he guest conducted at TCU's Daniel-Meyer Coliseum in 1964. For many years, he was NBC-TV's musical director, led the original orchestra for the *Today* show, and was the bandleader for *The Tonight Show* with Steve Allen. He picked up the baton again when Johnny Carson took over *The Tonight Show* in 1961. He played piano on Frank Sinatra and Bing Crosby's radio shows in the 1940s. Crosby gave Skitch his nickname based on Henderson's talent for quickly sketching out a musical score into another key.

OPPOSITE
Comedian George Jessel was an old-school entertainer who never strayed far from his vaudeville roots. Besides appearing on stage and in films in the 1920s and 30s, Jessel began producing film musicals in the 1940s and 50s. He had his own TV variety show in 1953 and guest starred on *The Jimmy Durante Show, The George Burns and Gracie Allen Show, The Jack Benny Program,* and *The Jackie Gleason Show.*

ABOVE
Johnny Desmond's singing career took off when he joined Bob Crosby's band, the Bob-o-Links, in 1940. Before working with Glenn Miller's Army Air Force Band during World War II, Desmond was the featured vocalist for Gene Krupa's band. He costarred in the 1961 summer TV replacement program *Glenn Miller Time*, which featured the late Glenn Miller's orchestra under the direction of Fort Worth bandleader Ray McKinley.

ABOVE
Actor George Maharis costarred with Martin Milner in the highly rated TV series *Route 66* for three seasons. Afterwards, he took a series of film roles, including in *The Happening* and *The Desperados,* and later returned to television as a guest star in *Night Gallery, Mission: Impossible,* and *Barnaby Jones,* among other shows.

ABOVE
Carol Lynley was active in dramatic anthology television, starting in 1956 with a number of parts in *Goodyear Television Playhouse, General Electric Theatre, The Alcoa Hour,* and *The Kaiser Aluminum Hour.* Her starring role in the Broadway production of *Blue Denim* brought her to the West Coast to star in the film version of the play, earning her a 1959 Golden Globe nomination for Most Promising Female Newcomer. Lynley returned in 1961 for *Return to Peyton Place,* followed by *The Last Sunset, The Stripper, Under the Yum Yum Tree,* and *The Pleasure Seekers,* among other films. In 1965, she starred in *Harlow* and *Bunny Lake is Missing.*

ABOVE RIGHT
Actor Anthony Perkins made the jump from TV into films with a costarring role in 1956's *Friendly Persuasion,* for which he received the Golden Globe for New Star of the Year and a supporting actor Academy Award nomination. More film roles followed, including in *The Lonely Man, The Tin Star, Fear Strikes Out, The Matchmaker, On the Beach,* and *Tall Story.* In spite of all of his acclaimed performances, it was impossible for Perkins to eclipse his 1960 Norman Bates role in Alfred Hitchcock's *Psycho.*

ABOVE
Before singing at the 1964 Texas Democratic Convention in Dallas, pop singer Julius La Rosa visited Channel 5 for an interview with me. La Rosa got his big show business break from Arthur Godfrey, who made him a regular on both of his star-making TV shows *Arthur Godfrey Time* and *Arthur Godfrey and His Friends.* He had his own television show, *The Julius La Rosa Show,* in the summers of 1955 through 1957.

ABOVE

To many filmgoers, British actor Michael Rennie will forever be the haunting alien visitor, Klaatu, from the 1951 science fiction movie *The Day the Earth Stood Still.* By the end of his thirty-five-year acting career, Rennie had more than fifty film credits to his name and had guest appearances in an equal number of television programs. His first screen appearance in 1936 was an uncredited one, in Alfred Hitchcock's *Secret Agent.* A career highlight for Rennie was his Harry Lime role in the television series *The Third Man,* which ran from 1959 until 1965.

ABOVE

When Barbara Eden appeared on *Dateline* in 1964, she had yet to go blonde and yet to be cast in *I Dream of Jeannie.* She had already amassed a long list of episodic television credits, including *Highway Patrol, I Love Lucy, The Millionaire, Perry Mason, Gunsmoke, December Bride, Bachelor Father, Father Knows Best, The Andy Griffith Show, Saints and Sinners, The Virginian, Burke's Law,* and *Route 66.*

LEFT

Austrian-born Maximilian Schell appeared on *Dateline* to talk about his starring role in *Judgment at Nuremberg* and about working with the legendary Spencer Tracy. Schell had been cast in *Playhouse 90*'s original live television production of *Judgment at Nuremberg,* which was later restaged as a major motion picture, with Schell reprising his role of a defense attorney. It earned him the Academy Award and the New York Film Critics award for Best Actor.

ABOVE
I never dreamed I would someday meet Bob Hope, one of the most popular stars on radio and TV, much less interview him multiple times for my TV show. I had been a big Bob Hope fan since listening to him on the radio as a young child.

RIGHT

Regarded as one of Hollywood's top male stars, Burt Lancaster came on *Dateline* to talk about his latest role in *The Train,* a World War II art-heist action film that featured Lancaster performing all of his own elaborate stunts. Lancaster won an Academy Award and Golden Globe in 1961 for his starring role in *Elmer Gantry.* In 1963, he won a BAFTA for his work in *The Birdman of Alcatraz.* Lancaster made a splashy screen debut in 1946 in *The Killers* with Ava Gardner, followed by three other film noir classics—*I Walk Alone; Sorry, Wrong Number;* and *Criss Cross.* He starred with Deborah Kerr in *From Here to Eternity,* which won Best Picture at the 1954 Academy Awards. Together with his agent, Lancaster produced a number of films, including *Marty,* which swept the 1956 Academy Awards and won the Cannes Palme D'Or.

LEFT

Don DeFore hit his stride in 1952 when he was cast as Ozzie and Harriet Nelson's next-door neighbor Erskin "Thorny" Thornberry in television's *The Adventures of Ozzie and Harriet.* In 1961, DeFore landed the costarring role of George "Mr. B." Baxter, employer of the live-in maid Hazel Burke, in the long-running television sitcom *Hazel.*

The *Dateline* interview with Pulitzer-Prize-winning playwright and novelist William Inge was a refreshing change of pace; Inge had just won two Academy Awards for his story and script of the film *Splendor in the Grass*. In the 1940s and 50s, Inge wrote a series of dramatic plays that became Broadway hits and were later successfully adapted to the screen, including *Come Back, Little Sheba*; *Picnic*; *Bus Stop*; and *The Dark at the Top of the Stairs*.

ABOVE RIGHT
Dr. Norman Vincent Peale wrote one of the best-selling inspirational books of all time, *The Power of Positive Thinking*, published in 1952. It helped make Peale one of the most influential spiritual leaders of the twentieth century. Despite the book's huge success, Peale had detractors, including mental health professionals who questioned his methods. An ordained Methodist minister, Dr. Peale changed affiliations to the Dutch Reformed Church in 1932 when he became the pastor at Marble Collegiate Church in New York City. He and his wife, Ruth, had a weekly television show *What's Your Problem?* where they answered viewers' letters. Peale also had a weekly radio show, *The Art of Living*.

ABOVE
Frank Mills pinch-hit on *Dateline* for an interview with hillbilly comedian Minnie Pearl. Pearl was a member of the *Grand Ole Opry* for more than fifty years. She guest-starred in ABC's live country music variety show *Ozark Jubilee* in the 1950s.

ABOVE

When John Gavin was interviewed by Bobbie, he was one of
Hollywood's most promising young actors. In 1959-1960, he starred
in a run of box office hits: *Imitation of Life, Spartacus,* and *Psycho.*
He was almost cast twice as James Bond, but lost out to Sean
Connery and Roger Moore. Gavin was later elected president of the
Screen Actors Guild and served as the US Ambassador to Mexico for
five years in the 1980s.

ABOVE

When Robert Taylor came on *Dateline* to promote his
new role as the narrator on TV's *Death Valley Days,*
it caused a flurry among the female employees
at Channel 5, who sneaked down to the set for a
chance to see the handsome leading man. Taylor
replaced Ronald Reagan on *Death Valley Days*
in 1965, when Reagan left the series to pursue a
career in politics. Taylor's screen career started in
1934 and ran through the 1950s, with a string of
notable film noirs in between, including *The Bribe,
The High Wall, Johnny Eager, Party Girl, Rogue Cop,*
and *Undercurrent.* He was subpoened and testified
against some of his fellow actors before the House
Committee on Un-American Activities in 1947.

LEFT

A television favorite, Ann B. Davis stopped by
Dateline in 1965 to promote the new TV sitcom
The John Forsythe Show, in which she had the
costarring role of gym teacher Miss Wilson. Davis
rose to prominence in 1955 with the girl Friday
role of Charmaine "Shultzy" Schultz in *The Bob
Cummings Show.* She received four Emmy nominations for Shultzy and won twice. Her biggest
TV role came in 1969 when *The Brady Bunch*
debuted, and America's most beloved housekeeper,
Alice Nelson, was born.

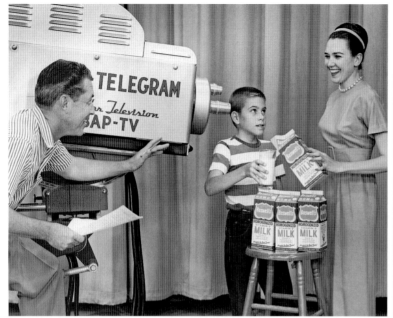

ABOVE LEFT
Another of my *Dateline* job duties was doing live commercials sandwiched in between guest interviews.

ABOVE RIGHT
When the Shrine Circus appeared on *Dateline*, I couldn't resist getting all dressed up. I am a self-professed clown lover who was once the only adult standing in a line of children waiting to get the autograph of Emmett Kelly, the world's most famous clown.

ABOVE
I visited Las Vegas in 1964 to file a series of stories from there for *Dateline*. Bobby Bixler (right), a Dallas public relations executive, handled all of Hope's appearances in Fort Worth and Dallas and was also the regional representative for the Las Vegas Dunes Hotel. Abe Shiller (left) was the Dunes publicist; the woman in the middle was a retired showgirl who worked as a Dunes publicity assistant.

ABOVE
On top of booking, writing, and appearing on *Dateline* five days a week, I was booked for speaking engagements throughout the community.

ABOVE
I interviewed Bob Hope during a rehearsal for his show at SMU's Moody Coliseum.

ABOVE RIGHT
More than one of my interviews with Bob Hope were on golf courses.

Shortly after I started hosting *Dateline*, I got a call from Bob Bixler. He said he represented Bob Hope and that Bob was coming to Dallas and would like to do an interview. Since we were the NBC affiliate, and Bob was on NBC, he thought we might be interested. I couldn't say "yes" fast enough. Bixler and Hope were in vaudeville together, but Bixler now did public relations work in Dallas and set up Bob's schedule when he was in Texas. Bixler didn't know he was talking to a lifelong Bob Hope fan.

The occasion was a stage show at Southern Methodist University Moody Coliseum. Bixler said Bob would like to meet us Saturday afternoon during a rehearsal break. As promotion director representing NBC, Phil went with me and my crew Billy Glover,

photographer, and Bruce Howard, sound engineer. For the interview Bob and I sat with our legs dangling over the edge of the stage, which was in the center of the coliseum. Bob was trying to get my name straight. He had met Phil. And I was Bobbie . . . long pause, as he fumbled trying to figure what my last name was. I hastened to bail him out. I said, "It's pronounced "WHY-gant."

He said, "I didn't know if that was your professional name."

I laughed and said, "Bob, it's my married name and my professional name. Nobody would choose 'Wygant' for a professional name."

He said, "Honey, if I can make it with this nose, you can make it with that name."

Not long after that, Bob and Dolores

Hope opened their Toluca Lake home in North Hollywood for a press gathering. In the backyard was one hole where Bob could practice drives and putts. He said, "Come on, Bobbie. Your turn."

"Bob, I'm in high heels and a tight skirt. Besides, I've never played golf." But he kept insisting, so I joined him.

He wrapped my hands around a club and said, "Just bring the club back over your shoulder and then swing it around to get the feel of the club."

I followed his instructions and holy cow! The club connected to the ball and sailed through the air landing about a foot from the pin. Bob immediately thinks it's a setup, a joke on him, that I'm actually the women's golf champion of Texas. I was almost on my knees explaining that it really was the first time I ever held a club in my hands.

Sizing up the spectators, Bob said, "Well, that does it. Tomorrow high heels on all my golf shoes!"

About half the interviews I did with Bob Hope were on golf courses. One time at Preston Trails Country Club in Dallas I arrived with photographer Bill Tippet to do an interview, but Bob decided he wanted to do it away from the clubhouse. So he hops into the driver's seat of a golf cart along with James "Jimmy" Chambers, publisher of the *Dallas Times Herald*. I was in the back seat, and the caddy was riding on the back with the clubs. Bob takes off with a big whoosh and heads across the green at a fast clip. All of a sudden there's a big drop-off, and it looks like we're about to be airborne. Were it not for the big, heavyset caddy who dragged his feet to steady the cart, we would have been in the trees. It could have been a disaster. Tippet, my photographer, kidded me about the headline. "Golf cart accident injures Bob Hope, publisher Jimmy Chambers, and, in small print, local TV personality." He laughed, "There's no way you can get billing with those

two in the cart!"

Celebrities came on *Dateline* regularly, but a few personal favorites stand out. I was thrilled to interview Paul Whiteman, the legendary orchestra leader who gave Bing Crosby his start when he hired three singers called The Rhythm Boys in 1926. Crosby was one of the three.

Following his winning the 1958 International Tchaikovsky Piano Competition in Moscow, Van Cliburn made his home in Fort Worth. Van came on the show and was happy to play the piano. This was just before the first Van Cliburn International Piano Competition in Fort Worth in 1962. There never was a more gracious, more generous person on the face of the earth than Van Cliburn.

Psychologist Dr. Joyce Brothers was a guest several times. She was an author and frequent guest on network television shows and had hosted her own TV show since 1958. My psychology studies at Purdue were a good background for these interviews and have been as valuable to my craft as any broadcast training I received. The two disciplines go hand in hand.

Ginger Rogers appeared several times. She talked about living in Fort Worth before she went to Hollywood. It was winning a dance contest in Fort Worth that led her to show business and eventually to movies. In one interview I asked her about dating Howard Hughes. She admitted they were friends but would give no details. She said, "I'm saving that for my book."

When Robert Goulet came on the show, he brought his fiancée Carol Lawrence, who was appearing with him at the Dallas Summer Musicals. Prior to the interview I was standing on a set next to them, doing a live commercial. When that ended I walked a few steps and sat next to Goulet. This was the day of the miniskirt. When I sat down the skirt started riding up. The director and I had an understanding that anytime this

OPPOSITE
Actress and dancer Ginger Rogers was booked on *Dateline* in 1963 while she was starring in *The Unsinkable Molly Brown* at the Dallas Summer Musicals. At the age of nine, Rogers moved to Fort Worth where she won a charleston contest, setting the course for her long, successful entertainment career. In 1933, she partnered with Fred Astaire for their first film together, *Flying Down to Rio*, which demonstrated the special connection between the iconic couple. Nine films together followed. Post-Astaire, Rogers proved to be a skillful screen actress in *Stage Door* and won the Academy Award for Best Actress in 1941 for her starring role in *Kitty Foyle*.

OPPOSITE
Piano virtuoso Van Cliburn appeared on *Dateline* in 1962, just before the first Van Cliburn International Piano Competition was held in Fort Worth. Cliburn emerged as a world-class superstar after winning the first International Tchaikovsky Piano Competition in Moscow in 1958. Welcomed back to the States with a ticker-tape parade in New York City, he ended up on the cover of *Time* magazine.

ABOVE
ABOVE
Psychologist Dr. Joyce Brothers first came to prominence in 1955 after becoming the first woman to win *The $64,000 Question*. In 1958, she became the host of a TV advice program in New York, launching a forty-year career that included syndicated TV shows and call-in radio. She made many guest appearances on network television and dispensed advice in both a daily newspaper column and a monthly column in *Good Housekeeping*. She is considered to be the mother of television pop psychology.

RIGHT
Big bandleader Paul Whiteman had a career comeback in the 1950s after being one of the biggest names in popular music in the 1920s and 1930s. He worked with such musical giants as Hoagy Carmichael, George Gershwin, Paul Robeson, and Billie Holiday. Known as "The King of Jazz," Whiteman had his own television variety show *Paul Whiteman's Goodyear Revue,* which ran from 1949 through 1952.

ABOVE
Stage actors and singers Robert Goulet and Carol Lawrence had not yet married when they came on *Dateline* in 1963. Goulet was best known for playing Sir Lancelot in the original stage production of the Broadway musical *Camelot*. Lawrence was known for her starring role as Maria in the original Broadway production of *West Side Story*.

RIGHT

TV-Radio Mirror, a nationally distributed monthly magazine in New York, gave me the star treatment in a 1964 feature profile that included photographs of me playing my favorite records.

RIGHT

Outtakes from the *TV-Radio Mirror* photo shoot include Phil and me relaxing in our living room.

happened, he would cut to a single shot of me while I adjusted my skirt and moved the floral arrangement to cover my legs. While all of this was going on Goulet, unseen by TV viewers, was mimicking me by pulling at his golf shorts. It was a hot summer day. While all of this was going on with the camera showing only me, I was ad-libbing an intro to my guests, concluding with "And while I am seated here pulling down my skirt Robert Goulet is seated next to me pulling down his shorts." The studio broke into pandemonium. The crew laughed uproariously. While we didn't usually have a studio audience, that day many of the staff drifted into the studio during lunch breaks to see Robert Goulet, who was the big hot male star of the day. Goulet played it to the hilt, while Carol Lawrence wasn't quite sure what was happening. I think we mentioned their show, but I wouldn't swear to it.

ABOVE
This redwood tiki sculpture we named George was part of the art collection Phil and I started amassing.

ABOVE RIGHT
Schlitz, beloved Dalmatian, was an important part of our home life. Schlitz lived to be seventeen.

RIGHT
Here I am dusting off my ski boots in preparation for another trip to Aspen.

FIVE

JFK

November 22, 1963, was my thirty-seventh birthday, but for Phil and me it was another day at the TV station. Since we both had November birthdays, we never planned big celebrations. We lumped our birthdays into Christmas. This November 22 was special, however, because President John F. Kennedy was coming to Fort Worth and Dallas.

OPPOSITE
The Hotel Texas marquee displays welcome greetings to President John F. Kennedy.

The station planned TV coverage of the president's appearance in the morning at the Hotel Texas in Fort Worth and later at a luncheon in the Dallas Trade Mart.

The station was not doing live coverage of the parade through downtown Dallas. Remember, this was 1963. Live coverage was not as flexible as it is now. News cameras were covering the parade on film. When I started my *Dateline* program at 12:30 p.m. that day I was instructed to tell the viewers, "When President Kennedy arrives at the Trade Mart for the luncheon, we will cut immediately to live coverage. So be aware that I may suddenly disappear."

Meanwhile I had two guests on the set for live interviews. The first was Ray McKinley, a native Fort Worthian and a famous bandleader who was appearing with his orchestra that night at the Casino Ballroom on Lake Worth. Before we went on, McKinley and Curly Broyles of our sales staff renewed their friendship. At one time Curly played trumpet with Ray's orchestra, and now Curly fronted his own group in addition to selling ad time for WBAP-TV.

Shortly after we started the on-air interview I noticed that the floor director, Ed Milner, was having a very animated discussion with director Sid Smith, who was in the control room. At the same time Ed was holding up his hands in a way that was not a standard hand signal for on-air people. In 1963 the talent did not wear headsets or earpieces. We had no contact with the control room.

All of a sudden I saw a slide on the monitor "NEWS BULLETIN." I stopped talking and heard Tom Whalen's off-camera voice saying that Bob Welch, our photographer at the Kennedy parade in Dallas, was reporting

TOP RIGHT
Despite the late hour, enthusiastic throngs of well-wishers greet the Kennedys.

ABOVE
After the short speech, Kennedy shakes hands with his Fort Worth fans.

TOP LEFT
The president's plane arrives at Fort Worth's Carswell Air Force Base at 11:07 p.m. on November 21, 1963. Texas Governor John Connally is on the left.

ABOVE
On November 22, 1963, at 8:45 a.m., President Kennedy goes outside the Hotel Texas to give unscheduled remarks to the people who have gathered in an open parking lot, even though it's drizzling. Behind him (left to right) state senator Don Kennard, Governor John Connally, and Vice President Lyndon Johnson.

Jackie Kennedy arrives at the breakfast at 9:20 a.m. and greets
Vice President Johnson. Fort Worth Chamber of Commerce
President Raymond Buck is on the far right of the photo.

ABOVE
President Kennedy and entourage depart the Hotel Texas at 10:35
a.m. to go back to Air Force One, which is waiting at Carswell Air
Force Base to fly to Dallas Love Field. The presidential entourage
includes US Congressman Jim Wright on the president's right and
Governor John Connally and his wife Nellie walking behind. Vice
President Johnson is on the president's left. US senator Ralph
Yarborough is on Wright's right.

TOP LEFT
At 9:00 a.m. President Kennedy goes back into the Hotel Texas
ballroom for the Fort Worth Chamber of Commerce Presidential
Breakfast attended by Vice President Johnson (center left)
and his wife Lady Bird (left).

ABOVE
President Kennedy delivers his scheduled speech
at the Chamber's breakfast at 9:25 a.m.

OPPOSITE
The Kennedys disembark from
Air Force One at Dallas Love Field
about 11:44 a.m.

ABOVE
Jackie Kennedy receives a dozen
red roses.

ABOVE RIGHT
The Kennedys disregard the
schedule and walk over to the Love
Field fence line to shake hands with
their supporters.

sounds, possibly shots, in the vicinity of the presidential motorcade. Whalen, who was a morning anchor, talking over the news bulletin slide, told viewers, "Stay tuned for more reports as we receive them." At the end of the brief announcement Ed Milner said to me, "We're coming back to you, Bobbie. Pick up where you left off."

When the camera came to me I said, "As soon as we get more information we'll interrupt this program, so stay with us." Then I turned to Ray McKinley, and we continued to talk about his being back in Fort Worth. I did not feel nervous or scared. I just wanted to pay close attention and be ready for whatever I might be called to do. For a fleeting moment I thought, "Some nut is shooting off firecrackers."

Since it was the noon hour, the newsroom was not at full staff, but the word quickly went out for everyone to get to the station. The interruptions came every minute or so over a news bulletin slide with Tom Whalen's

voice reporting the latest information coming from Bob Welch and Jimmy Darnell, our cameramen/reporters in Dallas. By this time they had followed the motorcade from the parade location in downtown Dallas to Parkland Hospital.

During one interruption, Frank Mills came on set and, sharing my microphone, told viewers not to call the station, that it only jammed the switchboard. He urged them to stay tuned to Channel 5 for the very latest and most complete information. Frank left, and I turned back to Ray McKinley. I was so grateful to McKinley for keeping his cool and hanging in with us.

As the news bulletins continued, we learned that both President Kennedy and John Connally had been shot. I was shocked and saddened by the reports, but I couldn't allow myself to dwell on those thoughts. I had to pay attention to my job and what I was instructed to do.

ABOVE
The Kennedys and the Connallys depart Dallas Love Field Airport at 11:52 a.m. on their way to the presidential parade through downtown Dallas and the Dallas Trade Mart luncheon.

LEFT
The 1961 black stretch Lincoln Continental carrying the Kennedys and the Connallys turns off Harwood Street onto Main Street in downtown Dallas at 12:21 p.m.

ABOVE RIGHT
Seconds after the shooting, chaos ensued outside the Texas School Book Depository at the corner of Elm and Houston Streets.

At about 12:50 p.m. I introduced our second guest, Lambuth Tomlinson of All Church Press, a company that published weekly bulletins and other materials for local churches. Being a man of faith, Mr. Tomlinson also remained calm and suggested we turn to prayer for God's help.

While our station was relaying reports from Fort Worth to NBC in New York, the WBAP-TV remote truck headed for Dallas. The station was thirty miles from Dallas on what is now Interstate 30. The engineers called the grey truck "The Grey Goose." Others referred to it as the bread truck. The three engineers on board were Tom Bedford, the driver with pedal to the metal, Johnny Smith, and I. N. "Red" Walker. Before they got halfway to Dallas the engine blew a cylinder, reducing the truck's speed to a crawl. Thanks to a few cylinders that hung on, the remote unit of the first television station in the Southwest, with *Fort Worth Star-Telegram* and WBAP-TV emblazoned in huge letters on its side panels, chugged and puffed its way to Parkland Hospital, where the wounded president and John Connally lay fighting for their lives. Between interruptions we carried on the interview. During the last interruption the reports were that President Kennedy had been given the last rites of the Roman Catholic Church. When the camera came back to me I said, "I too am Catholic, but we should not draw any conclusions from this announcement because it is customary to give the last rites when life might be threatened." With that I signed off at 12:59 p.m. As we went to a

LEFT
On the way to Dallas, the WBAP-TV remote truck's engine blew a cylinder but managed to limp into Dallas. The disabled truck kept broadcasting for the next three days while tethered to a tow truck.

station break, doctors at Parkland Hospital were declaring the president dead at one o'clock CST.

Our ten o'clock anchor Charles Murphy arrived and took over at 1 p.m., communicating with NBC anchor Frank McGee in New York, who announced the president's death a few minutes later.

Meanwhile in Dallas, an NBC producer assessed the pitiful sight of the WBAP-TV truck and called for a wrecker. For the next three days our remote truck was permanently attached to the tow truck. As the action moved to the Dallas County courthouse and Lee Harvey Oswald, here came the wrecker pulling the crippled WBAP-TV remote truck behind. Humiliating? Yes. But the news broadcasts continued from the immobilized "Grey Goose" and even won awards for excellent coverage.

Now that I was off the air, I stayed in the studio all afternoon watching a monitor and feeling the shock of this devastating news. About six o'clock, I went home. Neither Phil nor I had eaten lunch, so we fixed dinner while keeping our eyes and ears glued to the TV news. Around eleven, Phil went to bed. I sat up in bed still watching the news.

Normally the station signed off at midnight with film of the flag waving while a band played "The Star Spangled Banner." This night there was no sign-off or test pattern. Tom Pettit, NBC's reporter at the scene, and our reporters and technical people continued coverage of the assassination throughout the night and for nights to come.

I fell asleep at some point with the TV still on. The next morning I woke up around daybreak. As I was coming to with the TV news seeping into my consciousness, I remember thinking, "I had the most horrible dream that the president was killed in Dallas. Thank heaven it's only a dream." And then I came fully awake and there was the TV showing me the president was dead, and his body was back in Washington. That's when I lost it. I was no longer the professional broadcaster on duty. I, like millions of others, was a grieving American.

Later, and for years to come, viewers who were watching that day would ask me, "How in the world did you manage to keep those interviews going with one interruption after another?" The only answer I could give them was "my training." By then I had been doing live TV for fifteen years. Broadcasting was my major at Purdue. I often think that on camera, broadcasters are like trained animals. We're told to speak, we speak; to stop, we stop; to stand, we stand. We just do as we're told.

For the fiftieth anniversary of the JFK assassination, Paul Harral, a respected journalist, interviewed me for the *Fort Worth Magazine*. One of the questions was: "Were there any complaints about the way we handled that breaking news?" I told him if

ABOVE
In between news break interruptions about the unfolding crisis that was shaking the nation, I was instructed by WBAP-TV floor director Ed Milner (on left in silhouette) to continue my planned *Dateline* interviews until the program ended at 1:00 p.m.

there were, I never heard them. My peers commended my poise and presentation. When I had time to reflect, I realized that this would always be my most difficult time on live TV. If I could get through this, I could handle anything live TV could throw at me.

I remember thinking, what if during a broadcasting class at Purdue, the professor had said, "Here's the situation. You're on air doing an interview when an announcement interrupts that the president of the United States has been shot, and in between the news announcements, you're told to pick up the unrelated interview where you left off and continue. What would you do?"

My answer would have been, "I'm changing my major to home ec."

SIX

The Beatles

The 1963 holidays were more subdued than usual.
The Kennedy assassination was still daily news.
Then came 1964.

OPPOSITE
I attended the invitation-only
Beatles' press conference held a
few hours before their Dallas concert
on September 18, 1964. That's me,
half hidden, just left of center.

The Beatles' appearance on the Ed Sullivan TV Show February 9, 1964, was big news. The Beatles got the highest rating the *Ed Sullivan Show* ever had. Even bigger news locally was the announcement that the Beatles would appear seven months later, on September 18, in concert at the Memorial Auditorium in Dallas. Phil liked the Beatles, but I proclaimed myself as the Beatles' oldest groupie.

Several weeks before the concert I received an invitation to meet with the Beatles' press representatives in Dallas to apply for credentials to a Beatles press conference. It would precede the concert. I filled out the forms and talked briefly with the representatives. I felt as if they were scrutinizing me.

When the press credentials arrived by mail shortly before the concert, it stated specifically that the credentials were not transferrable. If at the last minute I could not attend, I could not give the credentials to anyone else. I did not have a ticket to the concert.

The night of the concert Phil drove me to Dallas Memorial Auditorium. Our arrangement was that he would come back about the time the concert was to start. If I was not waiting for him outside, he would assume I was staying for the concert and he would come back for me when the concert ended. Meanwhile, he would be meeting with a friend.

Our news department had a photographer covering the news conference, but since I

LEFT
Strict rules of conduct were established when the press conference began. Before addressing the Beatles, journalists were required to stand up and identify themselves and their media affiliations.

was in the program department, I attended by myself. Prior to the conference, in a large backstage meeting room, Derek, the tour manager, came out, and in his very British accent announced the press conference rules of conduct. When we wanted to ask a question, we should raise our hand and wait to be acknowledged. Then we should stand and address our question to the "Lads."

The "Lads" were introduced. They walked in and took seats behind a long table. A large assortment of film cameras rolled, and still cameras clicked away. The Beatles' manager, Brian Epstein, stood in the background. They all wore suits and ties. The Beatles had their signature floppy haircuts. They were a classy group.

The questions started. "What do you think about Texas?" "What kind of girl do you like?" The usual press conference trivia. About halfway through the conference, I raised my hand and was acknowledged. When I stood, the Lads in unison said, "Oh, we saw you on the telly today!" The Beatles were staying at the Cabana Motor Hotel on Stemmons Freeway, a very posh place for its time. I was flattered that they were watching our show from their suites at the Cabana. Then I posed my question. I said, "You fellows are the highest paid entertainers in show business today. When you made your first big money, what was the first luxury you bought for yourself?"

All four said, "Automobile."

ABOVE
All four Beatles took questions from the crowd. Front row (left to right) George Harrison, Paul McCartney, John Lennon, and Ringo Star. On the back row are Beatles manager Brian Epstein (right) and Beatles press officer Derek Taylor (center).

When I said, "What kind?" they yelled out "Bentley," "Rolls Royce," and "Lamborghini." I couldn't tell which car went with which Beatle.

While the conference was going on, the opening acts were on stage. At a prescribed time Derek ended the press conference, and I worked my way to the front of the room to thank Brian Epstein for including me in the press list. As you might expect, in 1964 not very many women were at the conference. He asked me if I was staying for the concert. I replied that I did not have a ticket. He took me by the arm and said, "Well then, you'll stay with me."

So there I was, standing next to Beatles Manager Brian Epstein at the foot of the stage looking up at the Beatles in concert. Was this really happening? The Beatles played a thirty-minute set that included "Twist and Shout" and "A Hard Day's Night." But the screams from the girls in the audience totally drowned out what was coming from the stage. It was deafening, like being next to a jet airplane ready for takeoff. They could have been playing "Jingle Bells."

Now fast forward to summer 2012, forty-eight years later. The Beatles returned to Dallas in the form of a tribute group called Rain. Their show of Beatles music was booked by the Dallas Summer Musicals. I was scheduled to interview the group at the Music Hall at Fair Park, where there was an exhibition of photographs taken by *Dallas Times Herald* photographer Andy Hanson during the Beatles' 1964 Dallas visit.

TOP
Beatles' press officer Derek Taylor (second from left, back row)
stands next to a security guard while Brian Epstein paces.

TOP
Beatles' personal assistant Neil Aspinall, who later became the head
of the Beatles' company Apple Corps, is standing in the back row to
the left of Brian Epstein.

ABOVE
Beatles' road manager Mal Evans, in glasses, is on the back row, far right.

ABOVE
As a post-press conference media dog pile begins to develop, Beatles' press officer Derek Taylor (standing, second from left) negotiates an exit strategy for the Fab Four.

While my photographer was setting up I started browsing the exhibition. Suddenly my eyes focused on one photograph of Paul McCartney surrounded by a few reporters. One person was wearing a jacket with a familiar-looking brooch. As I approached for a closer look, I literally gasped. The person wearing the jacket with the brooch and peering over the shoulder of a male reporter talking with Paul was me. I had never seen the picture, didn't know it existed. Immediately I started rewriting the story in my mind. I said, "We need to get Andy Hanson on the phone and see if he can come here to the Music Hall so I can interview him about this photograph." Fortunately we were able to reach Andy, and within thirty minutes he was there. I interviewed him about that picture and his recollections of the night the Beatles played in Dallas. Actually, in that photo I was not waiting to talk with Paul. I was trying to work my way past Paul to get to Brian Epstein to thank him for the press conference.

The Beatles play in front of a capacity crowd of ten thousand at Dallas's Memorial Auditorium, the only Texas stop on their 1964 world tour.

SEVEN

Press Trips

Prior to 1963, film companies counted on newspapers and the print media to help publicize their new releases. One way was to offer press junkets. I prefer to call them press trips.

OPPOSITE
In 1963, I became a frequent flier. As time went on, I flew somewhere almost every weekend on a press trip to interview stars. I've accrued more than two million frequent flier miles with Delta Airlines and an additional two million with American.

The studios would invite the print press to interview stars, directors, and writers. It might be on a set in Hollywood or on location where the movie was being filmed. The film companies in most cases would pay all expenses, including transportation, hotel, and meals. In exchange the press would write reports about the film and its stars. It didn't necessarily insure a favorable review, but that's the risk the film companies took. Occasionally in place of a press trip the studio would bring an actor or director to the city where the press person wrote.

When a few local TV stations started doing talk shows and interview segments in news programs that featured entertainment news, the film companies took notice. In 1963 Warner Bros. decided to include TV people in a press trip. Because of my *Dateline* talk show I was invited. We were about a dozen TV interviewers from major markets invited to go to Jackson Hole, Wyoming, for the premiere of *Spencer's Mountain*. It was the first time any studio had included TV journalists in a press trip.

We flew to Jackson Hole on a Braniff Airlines charter flight. Our accommodations were very comfortable cabins in a state park, two to a cabin. We didn't get individual interviews with the stars—Henry Fonda, Maureen O'Hara, James MacArthur, or with director Delmar Daves. Instead they all took part in a press conference attended by both TV and print press. Later, TV people received film highlights of the press conference to show on our local programs.

ABOVE

Carroll Baker looked every bit the Hollywood star at the international press premiere for *Cheyenne Autumn* at the Lincoln Theater in Cheyenne, Wyoming. This was one of two early press trips to Wyoming.

ABOVE LEFT

In a ceremony staged in Fort Laramie, Wyoming, during the *Cheyenne Autumn* press tour, actor James Stewart (second from right), who played Wyatt Earp, and his costar Carroll Baker, who played a Quaker school teacher, were officially adopted by the Northern Cheyenne Indian tribe.

CENTER LEFT

Ricardo Montalban was cast as Chief Little Wolf in *Cheyenne Autumn*. The $4 million Warner Bros. picture was loosely based on actual historical events surrounding the 1878-1879 exodus of the Northern Cheyenne from Oklahoma to Wyoming.

LEFT

Karl Malden played *Cheyenne Autumn*'s Captain Oscar Wessels. The film was the last western directed by the legendary John Ford.

ABOVE

Spencer's Mountain was my first press trip. A highlight was this mountaintop dedication ceremony on the actual Spencer's Mountain, which overlooks the town of Jackson Hole. Special guests and dignitaries who joined the actors at the ceremony included (back row, left to right) Jackson Hole mayor Henry Clissold, director Delmar Daves, US Senator Gale McGee, Governor Clifford Hansen, Arthur Godfrey, Maureen O'Hara, Mimsy Farmer, Art Linkletter, Henry Fonda, James MacArthur (behind Fonda), and Bronwyn FitzSimons (O'Hara's real-life daughter).

Whatever fantasies about Hollywood movie premieres I might have had were turned upside down when I attended the premiere in Jackson Hole, Wyoming. It was held in a small vintage movie house. No red carpet. No designer gowns. I wore my ski pants and parka. My seatmates were an Indian chief in full attire on one side and on the other side a lovely Indian maiden in native dress. Welcome to *Spencer's Mountain*, my first Hollywood premiere.

The biggest event to come out of that trip had nothing to do with the movie. After the press conference we were free until time to go to the premiere. One suggestion was to take a raft trip down the Snake River. There were seven or eight rafts of different sizes, each with its own captain. I was guided into one of the larger rafts, being careful not to drop the 16mm camera I borrowed from our news department. Mind you, I was not a photographer, but with a few quick instructions I was able to operate the camera.

We set off down the Snake River with our captain rowing through lively waters. We were the last raft. After about five minutes a smaller raft in front of us was swept to the side and collided with a branch hanging over the water. As if somebody punctured a balloon with a pin the raft deflated, dumping five foreign press men into the churning waters. Among them was Bertil Unger, a Swedish journalist who always wore a monocle in his left eye. He had a twin brother named Gustav, who wore a monocle in his right eye. Both Bertil and Gustav were members of the Hollywood Foreign Press Association. They helped form the Golden Globe Awards in 1944.

ABOVE
Two hundred fifty members of the international press attended the *Spencer's Mountain* premiere at the Teton Theatre in Jackson Hole, Wyoming. The premiere could not have been more low-key. I had been warned by the studio ahead of time to pack warm and casual clothing for the trip.

RIGHT

In between the weekend of scheduled *Spencer's Mountain* activities, the press was encouraged to take an extracurricular raft trip down the Snake River. It turned into a calamitous event that overshadowed the film's premiere.

Immediately our captain controlled our raft so we passengers could help retrieve our press mates, who were trying to swim toward us. My most vivid recollection was of Bertil, monocle in place, swimming toward us using his left arm, his right arm holding a camera above his head to keep it from getting wet. As Bertil thrashed his way to our raft, I threw down my movie camera and reached to help pull him aboard. That shows you I was not cut out to be a news photographer. When the action reached its peak, I tossed the camera aside and tried to help the victim. None of us was wearing a lifejacket. This was 1963, before laws required them.

As soon as he could, our captain beached our raft and ran back to see if he could help the other captain. One man was missing, an older gentleman from Spain. After very tense moments the two captains were able to locate him and pull him out of the water. It must have been thirty minutes or so before they returned to our raft carrying the nearly drowned man. They placed him in our raft next to me. It was a sunshiny day but cool in the shade. I was wearing a heavy, bulky, bright orange ski sweater. I took it off and wrapped the man in it. I was afraid he might go into shock. We rode another fifteen to twenty minutes in the raft before they could beach the raft again, get him into a car, and take him to a hospital. It was a close call, but he made it. Within minutes the story about a foreign press correspondent nearly drowning on a Snake River rafting trip hit the AP wires. It was the talk of the town—not exactly the kind of publicity Warner Bros. wanted for its *Spencer's Mountain* movie premiere.

LEFT
It's a Mad, Mad, Mad, Mad World was standup comedian Jonathan Winters's first motion-picture role. When I interviewed him in Los Angeles the day before the movie's premiere in November 1963, he had not yet seen the finished film. The star-studded cast and expert direction of Stanley Kramer helped to make the film a huge hit.

As if that wasn't enough to stir the publicists' ulcers, we went to the airport the next day to take our Braniff charter back to Dallas, only to learn that our charter plane had a mechanical malfunction, and they were waiting for a part to be flown in. The studio execs were trying to get as many journalists as possible on commercial flights to their final destinations, but some would have to wait and go on the charter. There was concern about how they were deciding who got to go commercial. Elston Brooks of the *Fort Worth Star-Telegram* spoke up, "It's decided by circulation numbers." Jack Gordon of the *Fort Worth Press*, the city's smaller paper, moaned, "That does it. Tomorrow night Slick Air Freight!"

In spite of the adverse reports from *Spencer's Mountain*, other studios gradually added TV journalists to their press trips. For its 1965 movie *The Great Race,* Warner Bros. invited TV press to its back lot for a day of interviews. Each interview was done in front of one of the vintage cars on a lavish set from the film. Jack Lemmon did his interviews in front of the car he drove in the race. This was the first of many interviews I would do with Lemmon, one of my favorite actors.

Tony Curtis, Natalie Wood, and director Blake Edwards all participated. Even producer Martin Jurow did interviews. Jurow had already produced *Breakfast at Tiffany's* and *The Pink Panther* and followed them up years later with *Terms of Endearment.* Marty was married to a Texan, so we hit it off from the get-go. When he retired from producing films, he and Erin-Jo returned to Texas, where we became friends.

ABOVE

The 1964 press tour for Warner Bros.' *The Incredible Mr. Limpet* was held at Florida's famed Weeki Wachee Springs State Park, featuring live mermaids. The event was billed as the world's first underwater movie premiere, and 250 members of the media were flown in chartered planes to watch the live-action/animated family film in the Weeki Wachee Underwater Theater.

RIGHT

Portable 35mm film projectors were installed in the underwater theater. Don Knotts, in his first starring film role, played Henry Limpet, who turns into a talking fish. Carole Cook costarred as his wife Bessie. Optional press activities included deep sea fishing, golf, or a covered-wagon-train ride to a nearby Seminole Indian village.

FAR LEFT
Tony Curtis did his *Great Race* interview in front of his $50,000 film car, the Leslie Special.

LEFT
Jack Lemmon, one of my favorite actors, sat in front of Professor Fate's Hannibal 8.

BELOW
For *The Great Race*, movie producer Martin Jurow teamed up for the third time with director Blake Edwards. Their two previous films together, *Breakfast at Tiffany's* and *The Pink Panther*, became classics.

ABOVE
A long-time collaborator with Blake Edwards, Henry Mancini provided the score for *The Great Race*. Mancini film scores included *Breakfast at Tiffany's, Hatari, Days of Wine and Roses, Charade, The Pink Panther,* and *A Shot in the Dark.*

ABOVE

The Secret of Santa Vittoria starred Anthony Quinn. I was one of the American media selected to be flown to Rome to visit the set and watch the movie being filmed.

ABOVE RIGHT

The press corps flew to Prague for *The ridge at Remagen*. *Remagen* stars (left to right) were Ben Gazzara, Matt Clark, and George Segal.

Not to be outdone, Carl Ferrazza, a highly respected publicist for United Artists, came up with the trip to top all trips—a tour of Europe that included four countries, with stops in Rome, Prague, Munich, and Amsterdam. The summer of 1968 our small group of ten TV press people visited locations of four films to be released by United Artists in 1969.

First stop was Rome, but we didn't stay in Rome. We were immediately bussed to a village in the hills outside Rome. The movie was *The Secret of Santa Vittoria*. Interviews were with Anthony Quinn and Virna Lisi. Watching Anna Magnani do a dramatic scene was a special treat. Our photographers for the entire trip were the Maysles brothers, Albert and David, who in later years became famous documentary filmmakers. Two of their most notable films were *Gimme Shelter* and *Grey Gardens*. The interviews were done in the town square of a medieval village. One of my most lasting memories was a dinner for the

stars and press served outdoors, overlooking the surrounding hills. I was seated across from Anthony Quinn and his wife, who was wearing a Pucci print dress. We hadn't seen these fashions yet in the US, but by the next year everybody was wearing multicolor Pucci prints or reasonable knock-offs.

I mention this social gathering of putting press and stars together because in later years, this commingling was discontinued. I think it was done to protect the stars from journalists who abused such occasions by treating them as continuations of the interviews rather than off-the-record social gatherings.

Second stop was Prague, Czechoslovakia, for location shooting of *The Bridge at Remagen*, a World War II story about the Allies trying to defend a bridge that the Germans were trying to destroy to prevent an Allied advance into Germany. The stars were George Segal, Robert Vaughn, Ben Gazzara, and Bradford Dillman. The bridge

was recreated by the movie set designers. The highlight of the day was watching the filming of a scene where the floor of the bridge opened and several horses were dropped into the river below. All the horses were fine, and men in the river downstream caught them and got them out of the water. I wonder if that scene could be executed that way in this day and age.

When we checked into the Prague hotel I came face to face with Garrick Utley of NBC News. I knew him from an appearance he and nine other NBC foreign correspondents made in Dallas-Fort Worth. As promotion director, Phil was in charge of them in DFW. Phil and

I also met with Garrick in Paris when he was based there for NBC. Garrick was startled to see me checking into a hotel in Prague. His opening line was, "Don't you know there might be a war breaking out here?" After I explained why I was in Prague, he said, "I'm meeting my translator for breakfast tomorrow morning. You're free to join us to get the latest information about what's going on here." He explained that Russians were already in the northern part of Czechoslovakia, claiming it was only training maneuvers. I met him and his translator the next morning and passed along his report to the United Artists people.

Several days after we left Prague, the film company was told in the middle of the night to evacuate immediately because the Russians had entered downtown Prague. The film company took what they could, but had to leave behind the World War II tanks and vehicles used in the movie. They fled to Germany, where they completed the film. Fortunately, the big climactic scenes at the bridge had been completed.

The next stop was Munich, Germany, for the movie *Hannibal Brooks*. It too had a World War II background with a British POW who was ordered to get a valuable elephant out of a German zoo. Our small group of TV journalists was taken to the Munich Zoo to observe the filming of a scene that included a tree catching fire. We were all huddled together in an area where we could safely watch. But just as the fire was ignited a gust of wind caused it to flame more than expected. Immediately we were directed to "move back! Move back!" When I stepped back I tripped over a camera bag left by one of the journalists, and down I went. I didn't hit my head, but I fell so hard on my backside that it shook me up. A United Artists representative quickly got a car and insisted I be taken to a doctor. The first doctor who examined me said it was the coccyx or tailbone. He then sent me across the street to another clinic for X-rays. The United Artists rep and one of the TV press people accompanied me. I could walk, but at times I would feel a very sharp pain in my lower back.

We were met by a German nurse, a large woman who had to be named Brunnhilde. She spoke no English, but her motions left no question as to what she wanted me to do. She put me in a small enclosure the size of a broom closet. She indicated that I should remove my clothes. I stripped to my bra and panties, but when she came back for me she yelled, "nein, nein" and indicated I should take off everything. I looked around but there was no robe, no towel. Nothing! She opened the door and motioned for me to follow her as she stomped ahead of me. But stop! She's going by the waiting room. The door is open, and my two male buddies are in there. Brunnhilde is looking angry and yelling at me. I wrap my arms around my bare torso and in a crouched position follow her past the open waiting room door into an X-ray room.

The diagnosis was the same as the one given by the first doctor. They gave me pain pills and the X-rays to show my doctor back home. I was dismissed. But first I had to once again follow Brunnhilde past the open door where my press buddy and the United Artists rep would be waiting for me. Ach Himmel!

Back in the car, on our way to the hotel where lunch was being served, I wanted to find out if they were in the waiting room the whole time. They said no, there was a coffee bar in the adjoining room and they spent all the time in there. Then I told them my Brunnhilde story, and they put on a show about how mad they were because they missed Bobbie's strip show.

P.S. to this story. When I took the X-rays to my doctor in Fort Worth, he sent them to an X-ray specialist who showed him that the Germans actually missed a small break in the sacrum, which was already healing. It had nothing to do with the coccyx.

Our final stop was Amsterdam, Holland, for *If It's Tuesday, This Must Be Belgium*. The story about a group of Americans touring various countries in Europe had a number of stars, including Suzanne Pleshette. The location we visited was a cheese market. We were actually extras in the scene. Since Amsterdam was our last stop, we fit the film perfectly as bedraggled Americans moving too fast from one stop to another, with stories about almost being engulfed in a war in Prague, being caught in a fire at the Munich Zoo, and my nude appearance at a German medical clinic.

ABOVE
The press interviews for *Sinful Davy* were held outdoors in County Wicklow, Ireland. *Davy* star Robert Morley welcomed the press group that was growing in numbers. I am fourth from the left.

LEFT
When we visited the set of *If It's Tuesday, This Must Be Belgium*, the press corps ended up being cast as extras in this scene shot at an outdoor market in Amsterdam. I am third from right.

ABOVE
When the weather turned chilly during his interview with me, Robert Morley lent me his suede jacket.

ABOVE RIGHT
During my interview with *Sinful Davy* director John Huston, he extended an invitation for me to visit his private estate, St. Clarens in County Galway. I went.

John Huston's 1969 film *Sinful Davy* for United Artists prompted a press trip to Dublin, Ireland. Our TV press group of ten to twelve was getting a little larger, but was still manageable. The interviews took place outdoors on location in County Wicklow, not far from Dublin. The idyllic setting was on a grassy hill above a sparkling lake. Even though it was summer, as the day progressed it got cool. When I sat down to do my interview with Robert Morley I was shivering. Morley said, "My darling, you're freezing." With that he took off his jacket and put it around me. Being a rather portly man, he could have fitted two Bobbies inside his jacket.

I carried around a tape recorder because I did interviews for a daily feature on WBAP radio, in addition to TV interviews. At the end of one scene I walked up to Director John Huston to tape an interview. Huston must have been at least 6 feet 2 inches tall. We had barely started when he said, "You'll be more comfortable if we sit down." With that he plopped his big frame into a grassy pillow, and we sat looking out over the crystal lake and talking about the film while the crew set up for the next scene. One of the things I brought up was his manor house in County Galway. I had read about it in a magazine and found it fascinating. He said, "You know so much about it I'd like for you to see it. Could you do that?"

It so happened Phil was joining me at the end of the press tour, and we were going to meet our friend Pauline O'Brien, who was with the Irish Tourist Board. After that we were getting a car and driver to travel around Ireland. One of our stops was County Galway.

Huston called to his secretary and told her to let the staff at County Galway know when we were coming and to show us everything in the place.

The following week our driver took us to St. Clarens, the name of the Huston estate. A charming Irish lady introduced herself and said she would show us around. We went up a wide staircase into a room as Margaret said, in tour-guide fashion, "This is Mr. Huston's master suite." Then she started pulling out drawers and pointing to neatly stacked apparel, saying, "These are his stockings and here is his underwear." With that I interrupted her. "Margaret, please. We don't want to invade Mr. Huston's privacy." She sweetly replied, "But my instructions were to show you everything."

After we toured the house she took us to the stables and Mr. Huston's library and office, built above the stables. It was fascinating. Beyond the stables were the ruins of an old castle. On the way back to the manor house she pointed to another house which she referred to as "the children's house." The children were Anjelica and Danny Huston, who now were working adult actors. As we went back to the house she said, "There is something else Mr. Huston wanted you to see, but very few people have seen it." She reached for a key on a peg and unlocked a door leading to a lower floor. We followed and were shown into what looked like a basement lounge. She unlocked another door and motioned us to enter a room lined with cabinets on all four walls. Through the glass panels we could see pre-Colombian sculptures stacked like cups and saucers, one close to another. Phil looked at me but was speechless. For some years he had been a student of the Mayan civilization. He couldn't believe what he was seeing.

We had made several trips to Mexico in the '50s and '60s, to the National Museum of Anthropology in Mexico City, and to Merida and Chichen Itza. Another year we arranged to go to Uxmal and Xlapak. This took us through a jungle to a very small colony of Mayans living as they lived centuries ago. As the driver steered the Jeep through a narrow tunnel of dense jungle growth, he told me that I was the first white woman he had taken back there. When I asked him why he agreed to take me, he said, "They told me your husband was a Mayan scholar and he would know if you could take it."

The main reason for going to this Maya colony was to see a pre-Columbian excavation which had been discovered recently and was in miraculous condition. The only sign of anything modern in the primitive colony was a pedal-operated sewing machine.

Huston had assembled his pre-Columbian collection before there was a ban on taking such pieces out of Mexico. Often they were given to him as gifts when he was making a film there. Some he purchased. Phil judged many of them to be museum quality.

Some years later, after Huston's death in 1987, I was interviewing his daughter Anjelica. During a break, while the crew was making technical adjustments, I told Anjelica about her father inviting us to see St. Clarens. When I said Margaret showed us around, in a very nostalgic voice she sighed and said, "Oh, Maggie." The property had been sold years ago to some Americans. I asked Anjelica if she knew what became of the pre-Colombian collection. She shook her head and said very softly and sadly, "I have no idea."

While the press trips were fabulous, there was more to them than fun. They were working trips. The interviews required a lot of preparation. This was before the internet and Google, so I had to do my own old-fashioned research. There were no helpers. The studios provided press kits with information about the film and its stars. The kits helped, but to get something unique and not studio cookie-cutter, we were on our own. We also had to keep our shows going. I produced *Dateline* as

OPPOSITE
Robert Stack recounted the adventures of filming *Is Paris Burning?* which was shot on location in Paris. The period film's plot centers on the liberation of Paris during World War II. With most of the cast being French, many of the scenes were shot in French and later dubbed in English. Stack had enjoyed a successful film career in the 1940s and 50s but is best known for his leading role in television's *The Untouchables*. In the 1980s, he became the host of TV's long-running *Unsolved Mysteries*.

ABOVE RIGHT

I traveled to New York in 1966 to interview French film director Rene Clement (center) and writer Dominique Lapierre (right) for their film *Is Paris Burning?* The French-American coproduction had a large ensemble cast that included big-name talent from both countries, including Jean Paul Belmondo, Charles Boyer, Leslie Caron, Alain Delon, Yves Montand, Simone Signoret, Kirk Douglas, Glenn Ford, Tony Perkins, Robert Stack, and Orson Wells.

RIGHT

Actress Melina Mercouri had a starring role as a bordello madam in *Gaily, Gaily*. The press trip for *Gaily* was held in Milwaukee, where parts of the movie, directed by Norman Jewison, were filmed. Mercouri came to her madam role easily, having starred as a prostitute in *Never on Sunday*, earning her the Best Actress award at the 1960 Cannes Film Festival and an Academy Award nomination.

ABOVE

The Lyric Theater in Los Angeles was the venue for the American press preview of *Valley of the Dolls*, now considered a cult classic. I interviewed Jacqueline Susann, who wrote the surprise best seller in 1966 and was paid $1.5 million by 20th Century Fox for the film rights.

ABOVE RIGHT

Sharon Tate's *Valley of the Dolls* role as Jennifer North earned her a Golden Globe nomination. Two years later, she and four others were murdered in her home by members of the Manson Family. Tate had invited Jacqueline Susann to come to dinner at her house that night, but Susann ended up not going at the last minute.

RIGHT

Patty Duke's salacious role in *Valley of the Dolls* was a big character departure for her after playing identical teenage cousins for four seasons in TV's *The Patty Duke Show*. Duke won the Academy Award for Best Actress when she was sixteen for her portrayal of Helen Keller in *The Miracle Worker*.

I interviewed Yul Brynner in New York in 1969 about his starring role in *The File of the Golden Goose.* Brynner was a busy actor, with two other feature films coming out a few months later: *The Madwoman of Chaillot* with Katharine Hepburn and *The Magic Christian* with Peter Sellers and Ringo Starr.

BELOW
Christopher Lee (center) played the villain in *The Man with the Golden Gun.* In real life, Lee was Ian Fleming's step-cousin. Herve Villechaize (left) played Lee's accomplice. Post-*Golden Gun*, Villechaize gained fame as a regular on TV's *Fantasy Island.*

ABOVE
The press preview for *The Man with the Golden Gun* was held at Pinewood Studios in the United Kingdom, where part of the film was shot. Replacing Sean Connery in the James Bond role was not an easy feat for the dapper Roger Moore. *The Man with the Golden Gun* was Moore's second Bond film.

ABOVE
WBAP-TV Sales Manager
Curly Broyles and I check
out Channel 5's new 2-inch
videotape equipment.

well as hosted it. In the beginning I still had to run the continuity department, so there were commercials and show intros to write and program rundowns to prepare. Things eased up a little later, when the station hired Dorothy Qualls to take over the continuity department.

The press trips usually were on weekends, so I'd leave after the noon show, fly to New York, Los Angeles, wherever. I'd return Sunday night and go home and stay up very late preparing for the Monday show. Or I would get back Sunday midnight, go directly to the station, and prepare Monday's story. Fortunately I've been blessed with generous amounts of energy, and I don't need eight hours of sleep to function efficiently.

As years rolled on, more entertainment reporters were included in the press trips—sometimes as many as thirty to thirty-five. This reduced the interview times to four or

five minutes. Generally, interviews were done in four and five-star hotels. You can't have A-list stars coming and going from cheap hotels. Each star had his or her own interview room. They were mini studios. In the early days there would be one camera focused on the star. If the reporter needed to be seen on camera asking the questions, the crew would move the camera at the end of the interview to film the reporter re-asking the questions. I always had to do what we called the "reverse questions." You can see this process in some of the early interviews on my web site, www.bobbiewygant.com. Within a few years they changed to two cameras per room.

Staying in luxury hotels was one of the perks of the press tours. We spent so many weekends at the Four Seasons Hotel in Beverly Hills, the staff knew us by name. They even knew our habits. Usually I preferred morning interviews, in spite of the fact that I am not a morning person, but I learned early on that by afternoon the stars were talked out. They were bored by the same questions that were asked over and over again. My routine was that I would have breakfast in my room at 6 a.m., and it would arrive exactly at 6 a.m.

Once when I was staying at the Four Seasons I had afternoon interviews scheduled, for some reason, so I decided to have room service breakfast at 8 a.m. instead of the usual 6 a.m. Exactly at 8 a.m. the waiter arrived. I let him in and he said, "Are you all right today?" I replied that I was fine. He kept fussing around getting everything set just so and talking the whole time. He said, "You were the subject of much talk in the kitchen this morning."

I thought that was strange so I said, "Why was that?"

He said, "We even called the front desk and asked about you."

By this time I was wide awake and said, "Whatever for?"

Finally he said, "You always have breakfast at 6 a.m. and we were afraid that you were sick and that maybe someone ought to check on you. And even though your breakfast card had 8 a.m., we were afraid that you might need help." Is it any wonder that of all the hotels we stayed in, the Four Seasons Beverly Hills was my favorite?

In the 1960s each trip featured only one movie. But gradually film companies got together, and we worked two movies in one weekend. Then it got to be three movies per weekend. We'd arrive late Friday afternoon, see one movie that night, and do those interviews the next morning. Saturday afternoon we'd do interviews for another movie that we had viewed in our towns before we came, then we'd see a third movie Saturday night and work those interviews Sunday. If we were working in Los Angeles, we'd have to leave the hotel by 3:30 p.m. to catch planes that would get us home that night so we could do our Monday shows on our home stations.

I can remember more than once in Los Angeles when interviews didn't end until 4 p.m. I'd arrive at the airport at 4:45, check my bag curbside, do an O. J. Simpson run through the airport, and both my bag and I would make a 5 p.m. departure. I didn't do it backwards, but like Ginger Rogers I did it in high heels!

Several times studios did week-long tours promoting upcoming films. I remember one time when five studios went in together for one full week in New York. I got exhausted just reading the itinerary. Essentially we were to see a movie every night and do the interviews the next day. The thing that raised a red flag for me was that each day we had to move to a different hotel. Whoa! I replied that I would do the first film in the first hotel, and then I was finished. I was not moving five times in one week. It caused quite a stir among the studios, but finally they decided that I could stay in the first hotel the entire time if I would do all of the movies. I was to keep it quiet, however. Later I found out two other reporters did the same thing.

The studio publicists worked out schedules to the nth degree, but one word from a star could put them in panic mode. Barbra Streisand decided to do her first TV press tour for regional journalists for *The Prince of Tides*. She and Nick Nolte did separate interviews. Barbra agreed to talk to a select group of about twelve to fifteen journalists. Since I represented a top-ten media market, I was included in this group. I didn't know what to expect, but she was very pleasant and cooperative. The film was well received, so Streisand was a happy camper, so happy that about halfway through the interviews she told the publicists she wanted to do the entire group. You've never seen such shuffling of papers and schedules to accommodate her request.

The Mirror Has Two Faces was another last-minute Streisand press trip scramble. The

LEFT
I interviewed Sylvester Stallone for the first *Rocky* movie in 1976.

OPPOSITE
Barbra Streisand, shown here on the set directing a scene from *The Prince of Tides*, was very particular about the staging of her press interviews, especially for *The Mirror Has Two Faces*.

© 1991 Columbia Pictures Industries, Inc. All rights reserved. Courtesty of Columbia Pictures.

interviews were to take place Saturday and Sunday in Los Angeles. Saturday interviews were for local LA press. When Streisand saw some of the interviews on the Los Angeles stations that night, she flipped. She thought they looked terrible, so she sent word that she and her people would come in Sunday and restage the room. The first interviewers were ready to start Sunday morning when Streisand arrived and started changing furniture, lights, and cameras. For the crew it was worse than starting from scratch. The interviews were delayed about ninety minutes. Since Sunday was a travel day, this caused pandemonium. Streisand was director as well as star of the movie. The word was out that she wasn't getting the enthusiastic response to *Mirror* she had hoped for. The moment I entered the room she started asking me what I thought about the film. I didn't want to get into that discussion, so I ignored her question and talked to the camera operators about the kinds of shots I needed. Then I sat down, and when the microphone was put in place, I signaled to the producer to start the clock. I had mixed feelings about the film, but I thought it was entertaining. The interview went well, but I knew she was going to insist I answer her question about liking the movie. Part of the interview would have been me talking, and I wanted Streisand talking. The moment I ended the interview I immediately removed the microphone, quickly got out of my seat, and raced for the door with Barbra calling out, "Bobbie, did you LIKE the movie?" As I exited the door I looked over my shoulder and said, "Barbra, relax. The movie will do great box office! Audiences will love it!"

From the first *Rocky* movie in 1976, I always enjoyed talking with Sylvester Stallone. I interviewed him for five of the *Rocky* movies. One Sunday in 1982 we had a press tour in New York for *Rambo First Blood*. It was time to start the interviews, but nothing was happening, even though we knew Stallone had arrived. Problem. He didn't like the room arrangement. The crew chief said that someone from Stallone's staff had approved it the day before, but he still wanted it changed. So again because of the late start on a travel day, we got shorter interviews and another frantic rush to the airport. One good thing about airport security checks since 9/11 is that they ended our O. J. Simpson runs through the airport. In high heels!

EIGHT

The Celebrity Explosion

In 1950, the most popular gift on nearly every American's wish list was a TV set. By then 3.8 million American households had TV sets. Ten years later the number grew to 45,750,000, and by 1970 TV sets in American homes totaled 59,500,000, with no signs of slowing down.

OPPOSITE
After almost seventy years in show business, comedian Jack Benny was considered one of entertainment's biggest talents. *The Jack Benny Show* began as a radio program in 1932, debuted as a television show in 1949, and was on the air until 1965. Benny sat down with me for an interview at the Stoneleigh Hotel in June 1966 to promote *An Hour and Sixty Minutes with Jack Benny,* which was at the Dallas Summer Musicals. Benny's costars for the two-week run were new singing discovery Wayne Newton and the juggling team of Benny Igor and George Rudenko.

One result of the upward spiral in the number of televisions in America was the unmistakable explosion of the cult of celebrity. Since the 1920s, celebrity status had been reserved for movie stars who lived in marble mansions in that magic land called Hollywood, but these movie celebrities were rarely seen off screen.

Then along came television, bringing its stars into our homes and even our bedrooms. The new phenomenon not only offered entertainment but also brought wars, race riots, and political conventions all up close and personal. Television created its own stars and made celebrities of people who were up to this time mostly unknown.

Viewers wanted to know more about these TV stars who came into their homes on a regular basis. Thus were born shows that reported on TV personalities. By 1981 the reports and interviews included in talk shows and news programs blossomed into daily, thirty-minute programs devoted entirely to entertainment. The first was *Entertainment Tonight.* Gradually movie stars began to join TV stars in these entertainment news shows. The celebrities were shown at work and at play, at home, and on the set. These shows were so successful with both fans and sponsors that each network or syndicate wanted its own entertainment news show. *Access Hollywood, Extra, Inside Edition,* and *Lifestyles of the Rich and Famous* all contributed to the celebrity explosion.

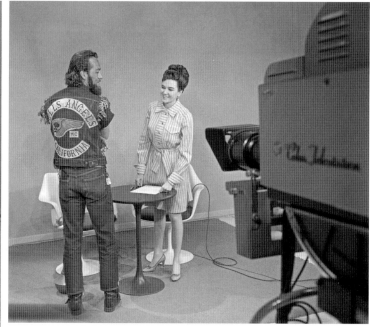

ABOVE
One of the most popular television comedians in the 1950s, George Gobel started out as a cowboy singer before turning to comedy. A master monologist, he called himself Lonesome George on *The George Gobel Show,* which debuted on NBC in 1954. Sporting a close-cropped crew cut, Gobel made a career of telling stories in a mild-mannered, self-effacing delivery. He was awarded an Emmy in 1955. When his TV show went off the air in 1960, Gobel guest-starred on television series and talk shows. In the 1970s, he became a regular panelist on *Hollywood Squares*.

ABOVE RIGHT
Sonny Barger, president of the Oakland chapter of the infamous motorcycle club Hells Angels, made for an unlikely *Dateline* booking. He was in Dallas to attend the southwestern premiere of the motion picture *Hells Angels on Wheels*, starring Adam Roarke and Jack Nicholson.

RIGHT
This is the script with my handwritten notes for Sonny Barger's appearance on *Dateline*.

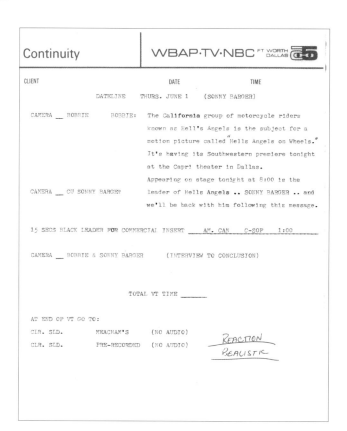

Continuity	WBAP·TV·NBC FT WORTH DALLAS 5

CLIENT   DATE   TIME
                  DATELINE   FRI NOV 24, 1967

BOBBIE ON CAMERA   BOBBIE: Last weekend we went to Houston to see
                                    Bob Hope, Phyllis Diller and Jack Jones in a
                                    benefit performance for Houston's St. Joseph
                                    Hospital.
                                    We took films of the show which we'll share
                                    with you after this message.

COMMERCIAL ___ AMERICAN CAN   C-SOF   1:00

CAMERA __ BOBBIE   (STAY ON BOBBIE ONLY 3-4 SECS)   THEN TO FILM

COLOR FILM ___ BOB HOPE SHOW   SILENT COLOR FILM   RECORDED MUSIC BG
                                  (BOBBIE NARRATES OVER FILM)

                            FILM RUNS 3:54
                            FILM IS CUED

AT END OF FILM ___
DIS TO BOBBIE   (BOBBIE TO END)

BOBBIE OFF AT 12:28:50

CLR. SLD.   MEACHAM'S   (NO AUDIO)

SHOW OFF AT 12:28:58

ABOVE
The *Dateline* script for my story about Bob Hope's star-studded show in Houston.

ABOVE RIGHT
Bob Hope flew in a cavalcade of stars, including Dorothy Lamour and Cary Grant, to appear with him at the Astrodome in Houston for a special benefit performance in 1970. Here he takes a short break from rehearsals to talk to me about the show.

RIGHT
I traveled to Boston to visit the set of *The Thomas Crown Affair* while the film was still in production. I interviewed actor Paul Burke on a polo field where Steve McQueen had just been filmed playing polo. Burke starred as Detective Adam Flint in *Naked City*, starred in the television series *Twelve O'Clock High*, and was the male lead in *Valley of the Dolls* in 1967.

ABOVE

Cliff Robertson was at the height of his career in 1968 when he visited me on *Dateline*. Robertson brought a red beret, like those worn in *The Devil's Brigade*, the World War II film he starred in with William Holden and Vince Edwards. That same year, Robertson played the intellectually challenged *Charly* and brought home the Oscar for best actor. He made his Broadway debut in William Inge's play *Picnic* and went on to star in films and television, notably as the lead in Playhouse 90's *The Days of Wine and Roses*. He won an Emmy for his role in a 1965 episode of *Bob Hope Presents the Chrysler Theatre*. Later in his career, Robertson became known to a new generation with his role in *Spider-Man* and its sequels.

ABOVE

Conductor Andre Previn was named the music director for the Houston Symphony Orchestra in 1967 and became the principal conductor of the London Symphony Orchestra in 1968. The German-born child prodigy pianist moved with his family to California just before the outbreak of World War II. He was given a position in MGM's music department when he was seventeen and by age nineteen had composed and scored his first motion picture. Previn, who made nearly forty jazz recordings, received four Oscars before he was thirty-five.

LEFT

Occasionally *Dateline* featured new cosmetic lines created by high-profile female stars, including actress and singer Polly Bergen. When she came on *Dateline* she talked about her new Oil of the Turtle cosmetic line. Bergen had a successful recording career starting in 1955 and released ten albums. She was the host of her own network show in 1957-1958 and was a popular game show panelist. She won an Emmy for her role in Playhouse 90's *The Helen Morgan Story* in 1958. In 1962 she starred with Gregory Peck and Robert Mitchum in *Cape Fear*. The following year she was nominated for a Golden Globe for Best Actress for her role in *The Caretakers*, with Robert Stack.

ABOVE

Singer Jack Jones came on *Dateline* in April 1969 to promote the opening of the Venetian Room in Dallas's Fairmont Hotel, where he was the headliner. Jones had his first hit single in 1962 with "Lollipops and Roses," which won him a Grammy; he earned a second Grammy in 1964 for "Wives and Lovers." In the 1960s and 70s he was a variety show staple. He sang the *Love Boat* theme song that opened the TV show every week for eight years.

ABOVE RIGHT

Comedic sensation Tiny Tim visited *Dateline* in 1969. His career exploded after his 1968 network debut on *Rowin & Martin's Laugh In*. Introduced by host Dan Rowan as The Toast of Greenwich Village, Tiny Tim launched into "A Tisket A Tasket," sung in his inimitable sweet falsetto with ukulele accompaniment. Endearing and disarming, he was an instant celebrity. Reprise Records quickly released his debut album *God Bless Tiny Tim,* which included his signature song "Tiptoe Through The Tulips." Before the year was out he had performed several more times on *Laugh In*, got married on the *Tonight Show*, and performed at London's Royal Albert Hall.

RIGHT

While William Shatner was in the iconic television series *Star Trek*, he released his first record album, which he shared with me on *Dateline* in 1968. *The Transformed Man* was a spoken-word record that featured Shatner dramatically interpreting current-day rock hit songs, including the Beatles' "Lucy in the Sky with Diamonds." A classically trained Shakespearean actor who performed at the Stratford Shakespeare Festival in Canada, Shatner's career highlights included starring roles in the television series *T.J. Hooker*, *Rescue 911*, and *The Practice*. His role in *Boston Legal* won him two Emmy Awards. He later revived his Captain Kirk character for seven *Star Trek* motion pictures.

ABOVE LEFT

When Nancy Sinatra called in sick for her *Dateline* interview in 1968, Lee Hazelwood covered for her by sporting a blonde wig and plugged their album *Nancy and Lee*. The record included the hit songs "Some Velvet Morning," a Hazelwood composition, and "Jackson." A country music legend, Hazelwood wrote and produced Sinatra's first hit song "These Boots Are Made for Walking" and also produced "Somethin' Stupid," the hit duet featuring Nancy and her father Frank.

ABOVE RIGHT

Actor Robert Young was on a nationwide fundraising campaign for Easter Seals when he stopped by *Dateline* in March 1970. After his interview with me, he recorded public service announcements at the station for Easter Seals. A few months later, Young won an Emmy for his leading role in the top-rated TV series *Marcus Welby, M.D.* In the 1950s, Young won three Emmy awards for his Jim Anderson character in *Father Knows Best*.

ABOVE

Actor Leif Erickson drove his RV into the Channel 5 studios for his *Dateline* appearance in 1970. Erickson was touring the country in support of his Big John Cannon role in the TV series *The High Chaparral*. He appeared in more than seventy motion pictures and numerous television series, including *Rawhide*, *Bonanza*, *Gunsmoke*, *Marcus Welby*, *The Rifleman*, and *The Rockford Files*.

RIGHT

Egyptian film actor Omar Sharif came on *Dateline* in 1970 to promote a contract bridge tournament in Dallas. The star of *Lawrence of Arabia*, *Doctor Zhivago*, and *Funny Girl* hoped to turn his passion for bridge into a high-stakes international spectator sport. In 1967, he organized the Omar Sharif Bridge Circus and invited world champion bridge teams to compete in exhibition matches throughout Europe. Thousands of spectators turned out to watch on TV monitors that displayed the bidding and cardplay. In 1970, Sharif helped to bring the Circus to seven US cities, including Dallas, home of the Dallas Aces, the world's first professional bridge team. Shariff explained to me it was an all-male tourney. When I asked why there were no women, he said women were not up to that kind of competition. I let him know I disagreed.

ABOVE RIGHT

The elegant actress Dina Merrill visited Channel 5 in 1970 to promote the new cosmetic line Amaranthe she created for Coty. Three times she was named to the World's Best Dressed List and finally made it to the Fashion Hall of Fame in 1966. She enjoyed a solid film career, notably in *Butterfield 8*, *The Young Savages*, *The Courtship of Eddie's Father*, *Operation Petticoat*, and *The Sundowners*.

ABOVE

When Phyllis George visited *Dateline* in 1970, she was the reigning Miss Texas 1970 and had not yet been crowned Miss America in 1971. In 1974, she became one of the first female network television sports commentators. She was a network game show panelist and in 1985 was named coanchor of the *CBS Morning News* but resigned eight months later.

ABOVE

Comedienne Edie Adams visited *Dateline* in 1970 to promote an upcoming NBC special. She was known for her impersonations of such actresses as Marilyn Monroe, Zsa Zsa Gabor, and Barbra Streisand. Adams, who had a vocal degree from Julliard and studied at the Actors Studio, became an integral part of the madcap series *The Ernie Kovacs Show* in 1951. In 1957, both she and Kovacs, whom she married in 1954, received Emmy nominations for best performances in a comedy series. She won a Tony for her role as Daisy Mae in Broadway's *Li'l Abner*, and played memorable film roles in *The Apartment*, *The Best Man*, and *It's a Mad, Mad, Mad World*.

ABOVE
I traveled to Los Angeles to interview actor Raymond Burr about his TV series *Ironside,* which was in the middle of its eight-year run. Burr received six Emmy nominations and two Golden Globe nominations for his portrayal of Robert T. Ironside. He won two Emmys for his starring role in *Perry Mason,* which ran from 1957 until 1966. In his early film career he was often cast as a heavy in film noir movies, including *Desperate, Raw Deal, Pitfall, Abandoned, Red Light,* and *His Kind of Woman,* culminating in Alfred Hitchcock's *Rear Window* in 1954.

ABOVE RIGHT
Comedian Flip Wilson was in the catbird's seat in 1971, with a hit TV series, an Emmy for Best Writing, a Golden Globe for Best Actor, and a Grammy for his comedy album *The Devil Made Me Buy This Dress. The Flip Wilson Show* premiered in 1970 and immediately went through the roof. During its five-year run, the variety show was nominated for eleven Emmys, winning twice. Wilson got his show business break with a *Tonight* show booking and returned there frequently, even guest hosting for Johnny Carson. He was also a regular guest on *The Ed Sullivan Show* and *Rowan & Martin's Laugh-In. Time* magazine proclaimed him "TV's first black superstar" when they put him on the cover of their January 31, 1972, issue.

OPPOSITE
Entertainer Carol Channing presented me with a Flip Wilson doll when she visited *Dateline* in December 1971. Channing was publicizing her upcoming guest star appearance on *The Flip Wilson Show.* Beloved for her Tony Award-winning role in the Broadway musical *Hello, Dolly!,* Channing was in Dallas for a three-week run of her nightclub act at the Venetian Room at the Fairmont Hotel. A special midnight show was added in the hotel's ballroom for New Year's Eve. Bright and early the next day, Channing was scheduled to be the first female Grand Marshall of the Cotton Bowl Festival Parade.

ABOVE
After making her first *Tonight Show* appearance in 1965, stand-up comedienne Joan Rivers was off and running on the TV variety show circuit with guest appearances on *The Ed Sullivan Show*, *The Mike Douglas Show*, and *The Dick Cavett Show*. When she visited *Dateline* in 1971, she was a semi-regular guest panelist on the daytime game show *Hollywood Squares*.

While WBAP-TV's *Dateline* was started in 1960 primarily as a fashion show to promote color TV and to sell color TV sets, it soon incorporated into its format entertainment news and celebrity interviews. I booked the show and did the rundown each day for the director. I had no assistant, no researcher, and no budget. We used to make a joke, "You've heard of low budget shows. Well, we're a no budget show." If I spent money to buy magazines to research an article about an upcoming guest, I paid for it and added it to my tax deductions.

My boss was Bob Gould, whose management style was to get the right person for the job and then back off and let him or her do that job. When needed, Bob would offer suggestions or pass along comments that might be helpful. Occasionally the sales manager or station manager would suggest someone for an interview. Otherwise I had full control of the guest list.

With press trips and stars coming through town we managed to have celebrities daily or at least weekly. I worked my contacts to know ahead of time when celebrities were coming to DFW. My interview style can be summed up as "Let's have a conversation." While I might ask a tough question and get into sensitive areas if it's what people were talking about, I tried never to blindside anyone. My mantra was never to ask a question I myself would not answer. I was not into gossip. I'd leave that to Louella Parsons and Hedda Hopper, two Hollywood columnists trying to outdo one another for juicy gossip.

ABOVE
Barbara Eden visited *Dateline* in 1971 when she was starring in *The Unsinkable Molly Brown*, her first stage appearance at the Dallas Summer Musicals. Eden had just come off a five-year run playing the leading role in the fantasy sitcom *I Dream of Jeannie*.

ABOVE

Peter Graves took a victory lap on *Dateline* after winning a 1971 Golden Globe for his portrayal of Jim Phelps in the popular action spy TV show *Mission Impossible*. The dashing actor, who was the real-life brother of *Gunsmoke*'s James Arness, starred on *Mission Impossible* for six seasons, as well as in the two-season revival of the program in the late 1980s. Graves is well-remembered as airline pilot Captain Clarence Oveur from the motion pictures *Airplane!* and *Airplane II: The Sequel*.

ABOVE RIGHT

Actor Arte Johnson established his career identity on the groundbreaking sketch comedy TV show *Rowan & Martin's Laugh-In*. When he visited *Dateline* in 1971, he had just left the top-ranked program and was embarking on a solo career that included supporting roles in motion pictures such as Robert Altman's *Nashville* and *Love at First Bite* with George Hamilton. He also made guest star appearances on television in *Night Gallery*, *The Partridge Family*, and *Fantasy Island*.

ABOVE

It turns out that Victor Sen Yung's role as Hop Sing, the Cartwright family's cook on TV's *Bonanza*, wasn't far off the mark. In his private life, Yung was an excellent chef who demonstrated his culinary skills on *Dateline* in 1971. The American-born Chinese actor played Jimmy Chan in ten Charlie Chan films starting in 1938. He appeared in more than seventy feature films and was active in episodic television from the 1950s through the 1970s.

ABOVE

Evangelist Billy Graham's *Dateline* visit in 1971 coincided with his ten-day crusade at Texas Stadium in Irving. It was the first event held in the massive new sports arena, with more than 43,000 people in attendance opening night and another 51,000 the following day. Considered one of the most powerful religious leaders in America, the Southern Baptist minister shared the gospel on his radio and television programs for sixty years.

ABOVE LEFT

After serving as the vice president of the United States from 1965 through 1969, Hubert Humphrey appeared on *Dateline*. He had unsuccessfully run for president against Richard Nixon in 1968 and campaigned for the Democratic presidential nomination in 1972, losing out to George McGovern. Humphrey's interview with me was during President Nixon's ongoing impeachment hearings, which Humphrey did not support.

ABOVE

Komar the Hindu Fakir demonstrated on a bed of nails the power of mind over matter. In 1971, he broke the Guinness Book of World Records for the longest time spent lying on a bed of nails, clocking in at twenty-five hours and twenty minutes. By day, Komar was Vernon Craig, who was the grounds keeper for the College of Wooster in Ohio and later managed a cheese and clock store. As Komar, he toured the world performing his unusual act.

ABOVE

One of America's most enduring singers, Johnny Mathis came on *Dateline* in 1972 to promote his album *Johnny Mathis in Person: Recorded Live in Las Vegas*. The set included many of his hits, including "Misty," "Chances Are," "Wonderful! Wonderful!," "The Twelfth of Never," "When Sunny Gets Blue," and "It's Not For Me To Say." One of Mathis's fans joined us on the set.

ABOVE RIGHT

Gifted actress Patricia Neal visited *Dateline* in 1973 to promote the British film *Baxter!* She made her first splash on the silver screen in 1951 in *The Day the Earth Stood Still*, followed by a memorable performance in *A Face in the Crowd*. She won a Best Actress Academy Award in 1963 for her role in *Hud*. After recovering from a debilitating stroke, she was nominated for an Oscar for *The Subject Was Roses* in 1968.

RIGHT

I interviewed Hollywood heavy Kirk Douglas in 1973 about his starring role in the TV movie *Dr. Jekyll and Mr. Hyde*, a musical adaptation of the Robert Louis Stevenson novel. Douglas was a well-established leading man with a long list of film credits beginning in the 1940s, including *The Strange Love of Martha Ivers*, *Champion*, *Young Man with a Horn*, *Ace in the Hole*, *The Bad and the Beautiful*, *Twenty Thousand Leagues under the Sea*, *Lust for Life*, *Spartacus*, *Lonely Are the Brave,* and *Seven Days in May*.

LEFT
Silent screen star Lillian Gish brought her self-penned book *Dorothy and Lillian Gish* to *Dateline* in 1973. Considered two of the greatest film stars of early American cinema, Lillian and her younger sister Dorothy started out in theater in the early 1900s and got their break into pictures after being introduced to D. W. Griffith by their friend, actress Mary Pickford. Lillian starred in many of Griffith's now classic silent films, including *The Birth of a Nation, Intolerance, Broken Blossoms*, and *Way Down East*. In 1971, Lillian Gish received a special Academy Award for her artistry and contributions to the motion picture industry.

Many guests had never spoken on radio, much less on TV. They would come in having been awake all night with stomachs churning like blenders. I would try to calm them down by saying if you can't talk, I'll talk for you. I would assure them, "You may think you're going to die but you'll live through this. I've never lost a guest."

I'm often asked if I get nervous with people I'm interviewing. The answer is no. Once I've done the homework for an interview, I'm relaxed and ready for the guest. I chuckle to myself at the idea of becoming intimidated, because my heritage is French-Irish. I'm not easily intimidated. I think I got that from my Irish Granddad Connolly and from my mother's French ancestry. She always told my brothers and me that we were as good as but no better than anyone else.

Lillian Gish, a silent film star who made the transition to "talkies," was a special interview for me. She recalled that in silent movies the stars had no stunt doubles. In the 1920 silent film *Way Down East,* Gish had to lie in freezing water at the top of Niagara Falls to get the shots for the big finish to the silent film.

RIGHT

Warren Beatty and Julie Christie caused a commotion on the *Dateline* set when they appeared on the program in 1971. The couple, who were famously romantically involved, were on a promotional tour for Robert Altman's *McCabe and Mrs. Miller*, a film that resulted in Christie's best actress Oscar. Beatty won his first Golden Globe in 1962 for his film role in *Splendor in the Grass*.

Warren Beatty and Julie Christie caused a stir in the studio when they came to DFW in 1971 to promote their movie *McCabe and Mrs. Miller*. When they stepped out of the limo, I noted that Julie was wearing a long vintage dress of some sort and was barefoot. When we got on the air she was holding something in her hands. It turned out to be some mending. She appeared to be darning something. Finally Warren said to her, "What *are* you doing?" She muttered something incoherent but carried on with her darning. I managed to get a few words out of her about her role in the movie. It was a memorable interview, but for all the wrong reasons. Later a local film rep claimed she had been smoking pot on the way from Dallas to our Fort Worth studio.

LEFT
Carol Burnett and Rock Hudson were starring in *I Do, I Do* at the Dallas Summer Musicals when they visited *Dateline* in 1974 . Their two-person show was the Emmy-award-winning actress's third time on the Summer Musicals stage, having starred there in her one-woman show *Carol Burnett in Person* in 1962, and again in 1963 in *Calamity Jane*. New to the musical theater, Rock Hudson was an established leading man in films like *Giant*, *The Magnificent Obsession*, and *Pillow Talk*, and was well-known to TV audiences as the costar of *McMillan & Wife*. After Dallas, the pair took *I Do, I Do* to the Kennedy Center in Washington, DC, and to the St. Louis Municipal Opera, where the show continued to break records at the box office. *People* magazine put the *I Do, I Do* couple on the cover of their July 15, 1974, issue.

The first time I interviewed Carol Burnett she was appearing in a one-woman show at the Dallas Summer Musicals. The crew and I went to her suite at the Stoneleigh Hotel in Dallas. When we arrived, an assistant invited us to go ahead and set up; Miss Burnett would join us soon. As we were doing microphone checks, Carol appeared all bright-eyed and bubbly. Her hair was in rollers surrounded by a strip of pink tulle. She sat down and I waited a bit, thinking the hairdresser would arrive and take down the rollers. But no. Carol said, "I'm ready if you're ready." I hope she didn't hear me gulp, but I began the interview trying to ignore the rollers. After the first question I had to address it. I said, "Carol, you are the first actress I've interviewed with her hair in rollers." Carol laughed that familiar laugh and said, "Oh yeah, this is my radar. I don't go anyplace without it."

An interesting thing happened while we were taking down the lights and packing the equipment. Carol got a phone call in the next room. When it ended we heard her say to her sister Chrissy in a very excited voice, "That was Joe. He's coming to see the show." There was more than excitement to the way she talked about it. It had to be a boyfriend. Later it turned out that it was Joe Hamilton, the man who later became her husband and the producer of her megahit, long-running Carol Burnett variety show.

Rock Hudson made several appearances on the show. One for a movie, one in Los Angeles for his NBC series *McMillan & Wife*, and another for his appearance with Carol Burnett in the musical *I Do, I Do* for the Dallas Summer Musicals. Rock was always charming and professional. When I talked with him in 1974, I gave him a hard time about something

ABOVE
The glamorous Hungarian-
American celebrity Zsa Zsa
Gabor appeared on *Dateline*
in 1970 to promote her new
cosmetics line Zsa Zsa,
carried by Neiman Marcus.

have to have a floor light." Normally we did not use floor lights. But she insisted. "Dahling, get them to bring a floor light."

So I said to the crew, "Please get her a floor light," which they did. Whew!

They put a microphone on her jacket lapel, but seconds before I was to introduce her, she said, "Dahling, vair is your microphone?" Mine was partially hidden inside my dress. I pointed to it and she said, "I vahnt mine inside," and with that she ripped open the jacket, exposing nothing but her bare bosom partially enclosed in a sexy, lacy bra.

I shot a look at the floor director that said, "Do what she wants." So between the red-faced floor director and Miss Gabor they managed to find someplace to clip the microphone out of sight. I started the introduction while she closed the jacket, and when the camera showed Zsa Zsa for the first time she was all aglow, thanks to her floor light and concealed microphone.

"Dahling," she cooed, "This is the most vonderful studio and I am so happy to be with you."

Authors were a staple on *Dateline*. I was always lugging a book or two with me everywhere I went because I read and made margin notes about the book for every author I interviewed. Often I would see the author interviewed on network shows that had researchers reading the books and writing questions for the reporter. One talk show host admitted he read only first and last chapters. I sometimes wondered if I really needed to read the entire book to get a good interview, but that question was answered when I talked with Bob Woodward about *All the President's Men,* which he coauthored with Carl Bernstein.

that happened to me in Aspen, Colorado. I showed up one morning to take a lesson with my favorite ski instructor, Bob Knight. This particular day I was told that Bob wasn't available. I'd have to go with another class, which I did. Skiing down a narrow run I saw Bob Knight ahead of me, and he motioned that I should ski on through. As I approached him I saw that he had a private student, and that student turned out to be Rock Hudson. So in the interview after recounting the Aspen story, I looked at Rock Hudson and I said, "I've got a bone to pick with you. You stole my ski instructor!"

When Zsa Zsa Gabor came to do an interview live on the set, she arrived shortly before airtime, looked at the set, and said, "I

ABOVE

Listening to America: A Traveler Rediscovers His Country was Bill Moyers's first published book. After graduating from the University of Texas, he received a Master of Divinity degree from Southwestern Baptist Theological Seminary in Fort Worth. He served as a top aide to Senator Lyndon Johnson during Johnson's bid for the Democratic nomination for president in 1960. In 1965, Moyers became Johnson's White House press secretary. A respected journalist and commentator, Moyer went on to have a long career in newspapers and television.

ABOVE LEFT

I welcomed to *Dateline* the venerated actress Helen Hayes (center) and renowned screenwriter/author Anita Loos (left) who were publicizing their collaborative memoir *Twice Over Lightly: New York Then and Now*. Often called the First Lady of the American Theatre, Hayes began acting in silent films in 1910 and received her first Academy Award in 1931 for her starring role in *The Sin of Madelon Claudet* and a second one in 1970 for her supporting role in *Airport*. She won four Tony Awards, including one for 1958's *Time Remembered*. Hayes's close friend Loos wrote hundreds of screenplays in her career, the most widely known being *Gentlemen Prefer Blondes*, written in 1925 using a series of character sketches she published in *Harper's Bazaar*.

ABOVE

Rod McKuen brought his thirteenth book of poetry *Come To Me In Silence* to *Dateline* in 1973. Emerging out of the 1960s San Francisco hippie scene, McKuen's poetry helped to fuel his already successful career as a pop songwriter, singer, and composer. He received Oscar nominations for his musical score and songwriting for *The Prime of Miss Jean Brodie* and *A Boy Named Charlie Brown* and won a Golden Globe for his song "Jean" in *The Prime of Miss Jean Brodie*.

RIGHT
Washington Post investigative journalist Bob Woodward autographed *All The President's Men* for me in 1974.

ABOVE
In my free time, I loved to ride my palamino horse Suzy.
I bought Suzy from my WBAP boss Bob Gould,
whose true passion was training horses.

ABOVE
Several department stores in Fort
Worth—especially Meacham's—
made sure I was always fashion-
forward. They provided many of my
on-air clothes, so I never wore the
same thing twice. Behind the driver
and me, waving from the back of
the parade wagon, are (left to right)
WBAP-TV's Bernie Tamayo, Bill
Kelley, and Bill Hix.

We did a longer than usual interview because I really got into the book. The one thing that kept coming up as I read it was that time after time, Woodward and Bernstein would get valuable, intimate information about Watergate and the people involved. But when they would ask the person, "Who told you that?" or "What is your source?" the informants would clam up. They would say, "I can't tell you that." So my question to Bob Woodward was, "Why would they tell you this secret information time and time again but refuse to divulge the source?" Bob Woodward said, "That is a very important question. I have been on every network and many local stations throughout the country, and you are the first interviewer to ask that question. I can tell you have read the book." Later Woodward and Bernstein learned that the people refused to name sources out of loyalty to President Nixon. When we looked at a playback of the tape, Woodward complimented me saying it was the best interview he had done. That's when I knew, "Yes, reading the entire book is worth the effort."

WBAP–TV CHANNEL 5
FIRST TELEVISION STATION IN TEXAS

FOUNDED BY AMON G. CARTER, NOTED PUBLISHER OF THE "FORT WORTH STAR–TELEGRAM", THE FIRST PROGRAM—A PUBLIC APPEARANCE, SEPT. 27, 1948, BY PRESIDENT HARRY TRUMAN—MADE TEXAS THE SIXTEENTH STATE IN THE NATION TO OPEN A COMMERCIAL STATION.

AMONG OTHER "FIRSTS" OF WBAP–TV ARE THE FIRST LIVE ENTERTAINMENT IN TEXAS ("FLYING X RANCHBOYS"), AND FIRST TEXAS COLORCAST VIA NBC–TV, 1954. TODAY CHANNEL 5 SERVES APPROXIMATELY 60 COUNTIES IN TEXAS AND OKLAHOMA.

SINCE ITS BIRTH, TELEVISION HAS MADE MANY ADVANCES. IN WASHINGTON, D.C., 1927, HERBERT HOOVER (AT THAT TIME SECRETARY OF COMMERCE) APPEARED ON THE FIRST MAJOR TELECAST IN THE NATION. IN 1931, H. & W. CORSET COMPANY IN NEW YORK CONDUCTED THE FIRST EXPERIMENTAL USE OF CLOSED–CIRCUIT TELEVISION TO DISPLAY ITS MODELS TO A BUYER AND SOLD $5,000 WORTH OF MERCHANDISE.

MODERN COMMERCIAL TELECASTING DID NOT BEGIN, HOWEVER, UNTIL 10 YEARS LATER, WHEN NEW YORK OPENED THE FIRST STATION IN THE COUNTRY. AFTER A SLOW START, MAJOR STRIDES WERE MADE IN 1947 AND 1948.

AS OF JULY 1, 1967, THE U. S. HAD 628 COMMERCIAL AND 128 EDUCATIONAL STATIONS, WITH 224 UNDER CONSTRUCTION. OF THESE, TEXAS HAD 49 COMMERCIAL AND 5 EDUCATIONAL STATIONS; 16 OTHERS WERE DUE TO BE COMPLETED SOON.

RECORDED TEXAS HISTORIC LANDMARK—1967

NINE

Big Changes

Fort Worth's Bob Schieffer is the first WBAP-TV alumnus to achieve success and fame at the network level. Schieffer and I first met in 1958, but it wasn't journalism that brought us together. It was acting!

OPPOSITE
A Texas state historical marker was erected in front of WBAP-TV's Broadcast Hill station in 1967.

One summer Dr. James Costy of the TCU Theater Department cast Bob as the young lieutenant in a comedy called *My Three Angels*. My husband Phil was also in the play as one of the angels. Occasionally I sat in on a rehearsal. That's how I first met Bob Schieffer. Dr. Costy knew Phil and me from our work with the Fort Worth Community Theater. While we both acted occasionally, we had no professional aspirations and were more interested in supporting a theater group for the city. Through the theater we also formed friendships that endure to this day.

Schieffer graduated from TCU with a degree in journalism in 1959. He served three years as a public information officer in the air force and in 1962 joined the *Fort Worth Star-Telegram*. In 1963 Schieffer scored a coup for the paper when he answered a phone call from a woman who was asking for a ride to Dallas because Lee Harvey Oswald, a suspect in the assassination of President Kennedy, was her son. Schieffer drove her to Dallas. At police headquarters he was mistaken for a detective and was able to gather information that other reporters didn't get. The *Fort Worth Star-Telegram* published four extras that day.

In another first, Schieffer was the first Texas reporter from a metropolitan newspaper to report the war from Vietnam. That was in 1965. I followed his reports with great interest. When he returned to Fort Worth I invited him to be on *Dateline*. Except for a news report with WBAP-TV reporter Jack Brown, this was Schieffer's first TV interview. He had taken many photographs in Vietnam and showed a number of them during our *Dateline* interview. He was so articulate and so at ease he impressed me very much.

ABOVE
As the Vietnam War continued to escalate,
Bob Schieffer convinced the *Star-Telegram*
to send him there to file firsthand reports on
Texas soldiers.

ABOVE
Bob Schieffer was hired to write for the *Fort Worth Star-Telegram* in 1962.
He became the paper's night police reporter and got one of the first big
scoops of his career on November 22, 1963.

RIGHT
Schieffer was the first Texas journalist from a metropolitan newspaper to go to Vietnam to report on the war.

FAR RIGHT
Soon after appearing on my *Dateline* program, Schieffer was hired by Channel 5 and named anchor of the *Texas News*

NEWS at SIX

with

Bob Schieffer

Weather Eye and Sportfolio

Monday-Friday

5 WBAP-TV NBC

COPYRIGHT © KXAS-TV/ NBC 5, ALL RIGHTS RESERVED.

BELOW
Bob Schieffer, shown here with sportscaster Bill Enis (left), was the first live on-air face for the nightly *Texas News*.

Bill Enis

Bob Schieffer

When it was over I said, "Have you ever thought about broadcast journalism?"

He said, "A little bit."

I said, "You're a natural for TV. Think about it."

Later I went to our news director, James A. Byron, and urged him to take a look at Schieffer's interview. Not long after that Schieffer joined our news department as a reporter and six o'clock anchor, as well as the first live anchor of the ten o'clock news.

Bob came on live and read the top news story of the day. Then the *Texas News* newsreel started, followed by weather and sports; Bob came back on camera live to close out the half hour. Prior to this, the *Texas News at 10* was just filmed news footage with an off-camera narrator. Bob Schieffer was with WBAP-TV from 1967 to 1969. In 1969 he took a job with Metromedia. That got him to Washington, DC. Soon thereafter he joined CBS News and became its chief Washington correspondent. Schieffer covered all the major beats for

CBS News and won all the awards and recognitions available, including the Walter Cronkite Award. He has been inducted into the Broadcasting and Cable Hall of Fame and the National Academy of Arts and Sciences Hall of Fame. Named a living legend by the Library of Congress, Schieffer hosted *Face the Nation* until 2015. In 2013, Texas Christian University named its journalism college the Bob Schieffer College of Communication. He is the author of three books, coauthor of another two, and still contributes political coverage and covers other special events for CBS.

In 1973 there was a rumor that WBAP-TV was going to be sold. This started after the FCC ruled that newspaper and broadcast properties in the same market cannot have the same ownership. Belo, owner of WFAA-TV and Radio and the *Dallas Morning News*, and the Times-Mirror Company, owner of KDFW-TV and the *Dallas Times Herald*, were

ABOVE LEFT
Channel 5's broadcasting signal reached sixty counties in Texas and Oklahoma in 1967.

ABOVE
An FCC Ruling forced Carter Publications to divest itself of WBAP-TV. On May 16, 1974, the FCC approved the sale of Channel 5, the number one television station in the Dallas/Fort Worth market, for $35 million to LIN Broadcasting Corporation of New York. WBAP-TV became KXAS-TV.

ABOVE
Doyle Vinson, news director of the
Texas News, climbs aboard an
Air and Space 18A model gyroplane
that the station used to film aerial
footage for news and sports events.

grandfathered by the FCC since they were competing companies. Even though Fort Worth had two newspapers, the *Fort Worth Press* wasn't affected because it did not own broadcast stations, but the FCC ruling forced the breakup of the *Fort Worth Star-Telegram* and its broadcast properties.

The WBAP-TV sale was on and off so many times the entire staff was on edge. Through the years my husband Phil had gone from TV director to TV production manager, and in 1958 he was promoted to promotion and public relations director. While the on again-off again sale was in play, station manager Roy Bacus told Phil not to make any vacation plans. Then came an announcement that the sale definitely was off. So Phil and I went to

Isla de Mujeres in Mexico's Yucatan for a week of R&R.

The Monday morning Phil returned to work, he met Bob Gould in the parking lot. Bob gave him the news. The station had been sold to LIN Broadcasting, and the *Fort Worth Star-Telegram*, WBAP-AM, and KSCS, the FM station, were sold to Capital Cities Communications. Carter Publications was no longer our parent company. LIN Broadcasting, our new station owner, was an eastern company. On May 16, 1974, WBAP-TV became KXAS-TV. When the new call letters were announced, the joke going around the station was, "These Eastern dudes don't know that in Texas that stands for 'Kicks Ass.'"

November 22, 1974

TO: ALL DEPARTMENT HEADS

FROM: BLAKE BYRNE

SUBJECT: FCC TELEGRAM

" Pursuant application dated 3/11/74 call sign WBAP-TV

changed to KXAS-TV effective as of 11/25/74. This telegram considered

part of the TV station license or construction permit until authorization

issued incorporating new call sign. " - E. Merle Glunt, Ass. C.E.

FCC.

As of 12:01 Sunday night we are KXAS-TV!!!!!

FAR LEFT
Among the biggest changes in 1974 was retiring the WBAP call letters and changing them to KXAS.

LEFT
LIN executive Blake Byrne was named the new station manager. After he moved to Fort Worth, things quickly changed at the station.

The first day the new LIN station manager, Blake Byrne, was in place at KXAS-TV, seven middle managers were dismissed. No reason was given except that they were being replaced. But this was only the beginning.

The LIN people decided that there would be no more *Dateline,* which by this time was a six-minute segment inside the Noon News. The entire half hour would be news. They would move me into the news department. I would no longer report to Bob Gould. With news anchor Chip Moody I would now coanchor a new half-hour program called *Inside Area 5* at 5 p.m. Monday through Friday. It would be a magazine format.

I knew Chip and liked him very much, but I didn't know how he would feel about cohosting with me. Furthermore, I didn't know how the rest of the newsroom would react to having me join them. Fortunately, I was friends with all of them. We frequently ate our sack lunches at the same table in what we called the "Chuck-o-mat" and later at the Chuck Wagon, which was a separate building from the studios.

As it turned out, Chip was the perfect coanchor. All he wanted were the hard news, sports, and flying stories. Chip was a pilot and aviation enthusiast. I could take the celebrity, entertainment, and arts features. From the get-go we had good chemistry and similar timing, which is very important. We both were quick on the uptake but didn't step on one another's lines. It was a very happy working relationship. Since I had produced *Dateline* for fifteen years, when I could,

Jack Gordon

New TV role for Bobbie to kill 'Dateline'

For 14 years, on what Channel 5 named "Dateline," Fort Worth's BOBBIE WYGANT has been interviewing the celebrities of the world in her own charming fashion.

"Dateline"—on from 12:20 to 12:30 p.m. daily and often on Sunday—became not only a showcase for Hollywood's Beautiful People, so brightly presented by Bobbie, but more—an institution in this area.

So it is with mixed emotions that KXAS-TV viewers receive the station's announcement: That Bobbie Wygant will do her last "Dateline" on Jan. 31, then on Feb. 3 is to move up as anchor person of Channel 5's half-hour weekday program, "Inside Area 5," seen from 5 to 5:30 p.m.

Still, all that is "Dateline" won't be lost.

"I'll still be doing some celebrity interviews on 'Inside Area 5,'" Bobbie said today.

DURING HER 14 YEARS with "Dateline" Bobbie figures she has interviewed all of 10,000 show business stars and other VIPs. Of them all, she has shared the air the most times with Bob Hope.

Bobbie has done interviews with Hope in the Fort Worth studio, in Hollywood, Europe, Australia. She once told the comedian:

"The only place I haven't interviewed you was in the men's room."

Cracked Hope: "The way unisex is going, who knows?"

Wygant interviews in Hollywood and around the world were filmed for later showings on "Dateline" in Fort Worth.

Some of her interviews have taken unexpectedly hilarious turns. Such as the day she had Buddy Hackett on "Dateline." Bobbie put one of her favorite interview questions to Hackett:

"If you could have anything in the world, money no object, what would you choose?"

HACKETT, A WILD MAN who always can be counted on for the unexpected, pointed to KXAS-TV cameraman Carey Simms who was shooting Bobbie's studio program that day.

Simms is young, handsome and of impressively athletic build.

"I'd choose that guy's body, if I could have anything in the world," Hackett answered, referring to Simms. "I'd use it as my own for two weeks, give it back to him, and it wouldn't be worth a damn."

Bobbie still laughs over the day she interviewed Robert Goulet at the studio for "Dateline." Somehow, Bobbie's skirt kept crawling above her knees. She tugged at it again and again.

BOBBIE WYGANT . . . she'll say goodbye to "Dateline" after Jan. 31 and become anchor for "Inside Area 5."

Bare knees were a no-no on the show, so the cameraman cut away from Bobbie to Goulet.

"Wouldyou believe it," Bobbie chortles, "Goulet was wearing walking shorts. And, as he sat, he was having more trouble keeping the shorts decent than I was with my creeping skirt!"

BOBBIE'S THOUSANDS of superstars interviewed for "Dateline" have included John Wayne, Johnny Carson, Clint Eastwood, Zsa Zsa Gabor, Gregory Peck, Liberace, Flip Wilson, Charlton Heston, the late Jack Benny.

Among other VIPs, Bobbie has interviewed Prince Rainier, Princess Grace, Hubert Humphrey, Julia and Tricia Nixon.

She has been named one of the nation's 10 top women broadcasters.

CHANGES TO GO INTO effect at Channel 5 on Monday, Feb. 3, will see a long familiar face depart from the station's High Noon News. He is admired, respected, will be missed—FRANK MILLS, taking early retirement. Moving into High Noon News on Feb. 3 will be Lee Elsesser and Sharon Noble.

After retirement at Channel 5, Mills will work as a freelance commercial announcer, he said.

DON'T MISS: Eight-foot-high illuminated statue of RONALD McDONALD, just installed on the lawn of McDonald's restaurant at 8600 Hwy. 80 West, at intersection with Las Vegas Trail. . . . In town from Hollywood, visiting Fort Worth friends: Actor NORMAN ALDEN. He was at Century II Club yesterday.

ABOVE LEFT

I was trasferred to the KXAS News Department, where I joined news anchor Chip Moody (above) to coanchor a half-hour magazine format program called *Inside Area 5*.

I assisted Margaret Megard, the *Inside Area 5* producer. While I was reluctant at first, moving to the news department was the best career move I ever made. Clint Bourland, the 5 p.m. producer, and Tom McDonald, chief editor, guided me through the transition. It was like going from a bachelor's degree to a master's.

News Director James A. Byron retired in September 1974. Russ Thornton, a longtime news department stalwart, moved upstairs to be Blake Byrne's special assistant. Lee Elsesser became news director. Lee was a "do everything" guy in the newsroom. Reporter, anchor, producer, writer, editor. Lee came from the Columbia University School of Journalism. He and photographer Bob Welch did a series called *Texas 70* in which they traveled the length and breadth of Texas doing thirty-minute programs that were excellent in every way—content, writing, photography, editing, presentation. They were A-plus on all counts. But apparently LIN decided that *Texas 70* was a luxury they couldn't afford. They cancelled it. Elsesser and Welch were crushed, as was the entire newsroom.

ABOVE LEFT
Chip and I worked well together, with me covering the entertainment and arts stories.

ABOVE
Chip Moody preferred the hard news and sports stories.

ABOVE
Channel 5 management devised the new *Texas News* slogan "Live on Five," in response to the rapidly changing news gathering technology that was revolutionizing how news was presented. With videotape replacing film and microwave equipment becoming smaller and less costly, live news reports from reporters in the field were no longer special events.

OPPOSITE
The *Texas News* was consistently the highest-rated news program in the Dallas-Fort Worth market until the mid-1970s. The lead anchors were Russ Bloxom (center left) and Ward Andrews (center right). Meteorologist Harold Taft is at the weather map on the far right.

ABOVE LEFT
The 1974 *Texas News* team: (left to right) sportscaster Boyd Matson, anchor Chip Moody, anchor Ward Andrews, anchor Russ Bloxom, and meteorologist Harold Taft.

ABOVE RIGHT
Phil grew up sailing on Michigan lakes, so when we moved to Texas, we saved up enough money to buy *Good Grief*, a thirty-five-foot Chris Craft cabin cruiser where we spent all our free weekends.

From the day that LIN Broadcasting was announced as the new owner, Phil knew that his job was in jeopardy. Even so, the day the axe fell, Phil was caught off guard. It was New Year's Eve 1974. Most of the staff left early, but Phil was still in his office clearing up a few details. He saw Blake Byrne go by his door, and then in a second Blake came back. He said, "Oh Phil, I've been wanting to tell you that I have a guy I worked with in Rhode Island coming in three weeks. You can stay until then or you can leave anytime you wish." Phil said, "Tomorrow is New Year's Day. I'll come in and clean out my office and that will be it." Blake said, "That's fine." And with that, Blake left. So much for twenty-seven years as a loyal employee.

Several weeks later Phil received a call from the office of Amon Carter Jr., who succeeded his father as publisher of the *Fort Worth Star-Telegram* after Amon Carter Sr. died. An appointment was made for Phil to meet with Amon Jr., who was very upset with the way LIN was treating some of the longtime employees. Carter said that LIN had assured him that employees would keep their jobs. When Mr. Carter found out what they were offering Phil for severance, he became angry and called Donald Pels, LIN president and CEO, in New York. He told Pels's secretary that he would be in Mr. Pels's office in New York Tuesday morning, and he expected a meeting. Some weeks later Phil was offered a more acceptable severance.

It was a restless time. New management. People leaving. New technology. In 1976 some of Channel 5 news was still shot on 16mm film, and some was shot with new minicams using ¾ inch videotape. Gradually, with microwave transmission, the minicam brought live reports.

Entertainment reporting was getting more popular all the time. *People* magazine debuted in 1974. Locally, WFAA-TV premiered *PM Magazine* with Leeza Gibbons in 1976. It was a thirty-minute Monday through Friday program featuring celebrities and

RIGHT

I met Freddie Prinze in Burbank when he was making the rounds at NBC Week during the summer of 1974. We talked about the twenty-year-old comedian's upcoming television debut in the sitcom *Chico and the Man*. The first network Mexican American television series, *Chico and the Man* was in the top ten for its first two seasons. Prinze committed suicide in the middle of the third season, but the *Chico* series continued for another season without him.

entertainment reports.

Press trips continued to be the primary source for my celebrity interviews. In 1975 United Artists took about a dozen reporters from around the country to Munich, Germany, for a location shoot of *Rollerball*. I'm smiling as I write this, because *Rollerball* was a science-fiction story set in the twenty-first century, 2018. It was a peaceful world except for the violence between the corporation-controlled rollerball teams, a combination of roller derby, football, and hockey. James Caan played a champion skater in a very violent sport. We spent most of a day at a roller rink in Munich watching Caan and other actors going round and round the oval rink. James Caan looked good, but his most difficult scenes were yet to come. I had interviewed *Rollerball*'s director, Norman Jewison, previously for *The Thomas Crown Affair* with Steve McQueen in 1968 and *Fiddler on the Roof* in 1971. There were many more interviews to come. Jewison and I were the same age. As time went on we laughed about growing older together.

ABOVE LEFT

Radio personality Wolfman Jack dropped by *Dateline* in May 1973 to talk about *The Midnight Special*, a pioneer late-night television variety show that featured popular musical acts and occasional comedians. Wolfman was the show's announcer and a rotating host. He developed his Wolfman persona when he started broadcasting a rock and roll program in 1963 on XERF-AM, a Mexican border blaster radio station that had one of the most powerful signals in North America. Wolfman made a cameo appearance playing himself in George Lucas's *American Graffiti*.

ABOVE RIGHT

Song and dance man Joel Grey brought his nightclub act to Dallas for a two-week run at the Fairmont's Venetian Room at the beginning of 1973. Just days before his interview with me, he won a Golden Globe award for his supporting role in the motion picture *Cabaret*. Two months later, he took home the Oscar. He won a Tony in 1966 for the same role in the original Broadway production of *Cabaret*.

ABOVE

Shelley Fabares appeared on *Dateline* in 1973 to promote *The Brian Keith Show*, which portrayed Keith and Fabares as father-and-daughter pediatricians. Fabares found stardom as a teenager, playing Donna Reed's daughter on *The Donna Reed Show* and recording a number-one hit single, "Johnny Angel," in 1962. She costarred in three Elvis movies and was nominated twice for an Emmy for her role in the sitcom *Coach*, which ran for nine seasons.

ABOVE

One of Hollywood's greatest performers, Gene Kelly received standing ovations at the Dallas Summer Musicals' production of *Take Me Along* in 1974. I caught up with the dancer and choreographer at an opening night celebration. Kelly's film career peaked during the golden age of the film musical in the 1940s and 50s. He was nominated for a Best Actor Academy Award in 1945 for *Anchors Aweigh* but is best remembered for his breathtaking dancing and choreography in 1951's *An American in Paris* and 1952's *Singin' in the Rain*.

ABOVE RIGHT

Distinguished actor Joseph Cotten visited *Dateline* in 1974 to promote *The Reluctant Debutante,* which he and his wife, British actress Patricia Medina, were performing in at the Country Dinner Playhouse in Dallas. Cotten's acting career began on the stage, notably as the lead in the original 1939 Broadway production of *The Philadelphia Story,* opposite Katharine Hepburn. He was an inaugural member of Orson Welles's Mercury Theatre company and costarred in *Citizen Kane. The Third Man* is one of his most memorable starring roles.

ABOVE

Television journalist Dan Rather appeared on *Dateline* in 1974 during a publicity tour for his first book *The Palace Guard*, an account of Watergate and the Nixon White House. Rather joined CBS News in 1962, and in 1981 replaced Walter Cronkite as the anchor of the CBS Evening News, a position he held for twenty-four years.

ABOVE LEFT
Best-selling country singer Charlie Pride was in the prime of his trailblazing career when he appeared on *Dateline* in 1974. Later that year he was voted Favorite Male Artist at the American Music Awards. He won Country Music Association awards for Entertainer of the Year and Best Male Vocalist in 1971, and in 1972 took home two Grammy awards and another Best Male Vocalist award from the Country Music Association.

ABOVE
Miss Peggy Lee came on *Dateline* in 1975 before her performance at the Dallas Symphony Orchestra's benefit Diamond Ball. The much-heralded vocalist sang on the Academy Awards show in 1974, performing "The Way We Were," which ended up winning for Best Original Song. Lee scored her first number-one record "Somebody Else Is Taking My Place" in 1942 when she was singing with the Benny Goodman Orchestra. Many hits followed. Her most famous recording is "Fever," released in 1958. She won her first Grammy in 1970 for her rendition of "Is That All There Is?"

LEFT
Milton "Mr. Television" Berle stopped by *Dateline* in 1974 to plug his eight-night engagement at the Venetian Room in Dallas's Fairmont Hotel. The show business veteran was still at it, with guest-starring roles on television and in movies.

ABOVE

I booked Academy Award winning actor George C. Scott and his wife, actress Trish Van Devere, to talk about their film *The Savage Is Loose*. Scott produced, directed, and starred in the R-rated period melodrama. Van Devere played his wife in the controversial film about an island-marooned couple. Ever the iconoclast, Scott famously refused to accept his 1962 Academy Award for *The Hustler* and refused again when he won for *Patton*, referring to the awards as a "meat parade."

RIGHT

I caught up with Chevy Chase in Burbank during NBC Week in July 1976 to talk about the upcoming second season of *Saturday Night Live*. After creating the "Weekend Update" franchise and winning two Emmys, Chase left the show mid-season in 1976 and went on to star in TV specials and a series of blockbuster films including *Foul Play*, *Caddyshack*, and five *National Lampoon's Vacation* films.

ABOVE
In 1975, I was invited to fly to Germany to interview actor James Caan (left) and director Norman Jewison while they were filming *Rollerball*.

ABOVE
I interviewed Sylvester Stallone in 1976 for *Rocky*. After writing the *Rocky* screenplay, Stallone convinced the film's producers he should star in it even though he had only minor acting experience. It was a big gamble but paid off enormously and developed into a well-oiled franchise.

In 1976 there was excitement about the trip to Los Angeles for the press premiere of *Rocky*. This was the first *Rocky* movie. Sylvester Stallone fought hard to get the starring role in the film, which he wrote. He even turned down big money for other actors to play Rocky. Finally producers Irwin Winkler and Robert Chartoff, director John Avildsen, and Universal Pictures agreed to let Stallone be Rocky. Stallone was plying the press with charm, humor, and cooperation. The majority of the press enjoyed the film and predicted it would be big box office, but I don't think anyone was predicting seven Academy Award nominations and three Oscar wins: Best Picture, Director, and Editor. I don't think Stallone himself could see five sequels in the future. One of my most vivid memories of that *Rocky* press premiere was Stallone's first wife Sasha. They divorced later, but that day she was the official photographer recording every movement with a 35mm still camera. Another memory was that our TV press group was growing. The dozen or so usual suspects had increased to about twenty.

Back at the station, the *Inside Area 5* magazine show with Chip Moody and me was getting good ratings, but overall the ratings for our news programs were falling, and if the ratings were falling the revenue was falling. Chip kept trying to get the 6 p.m. news producer to give us some hard news to lead the show, but the 6 p.m. producer and writers said they were too busy getting their show together to bother with the 5 p.m. show. So Chip would pull a still picture or two of the day's top stories and put that at the top of *Inside Area 5*.

LEFT
The 1974 *Texas News* team:
(left to right) sportscaster
Doug Vair, anchors Chip Moody,
Ward Andrews, Russ Bloxom,
and meteorologist Harold Taft.

Then one day in 1977, a rumor circulated that the 5 p.m. show was changing to thirty minutes of hard news. As soon as I could I went to News Director Lee Elsesser and said, "I don't know if I'm on a long list or a short list to anchor the new 5 p.m. news show, but my wish is that I not be on either list."

Elsesser looked shocked and said, "Sit down. I have reporters in here every day begging to anchor a show and you're telling me you don't want to anchor."

I said, "Lee, I'm not in any position to tell you what I will or won't do, but I'm saying that I can be more valuable to you in other ways." With that I explained that other major markets were putting entertainment segments in their early evening news shows and that I'd like to produce and host a five-minute segment in the new 5 p.m. show featuring celebrity interviews and entertainment news.

His eyes lit up and he said, "Let me run it by Upstairs."

A couple of days later he told me "Upstairs," meaning management and sales, "think that's a good idea. Can you start Monday?" So that Friday Chip and I said goodbye to *Inside Area 5*. The hard news nobody had time to do for 5 p.m. on Friday suddenly found time to produce for 5 p.m. the following Monday.

I embarked on a new phase of my career. In addition to celebrity interviews, I started reviewing movies. This made me the first film reviewer on television in the Southwest. In the 1960s I did reviews of Casa Mañana's live musicals and the Dallas Summer Musicals stage shows following opening nights. The drill was: see the show, rush back to the studio and write as much as time permitted, and go on the air as a part of *Alex Burton's Midnight News*. When I didn't have time to write, I adlibbed. *The Midnight News* had to be the most unorthodox newscast of all time. Alex read the news from an Eames lounge chair.

RIGHT

RIGHT

In an interview with me for 1976's *The Duchess and the Dirtwater Fox*, actress Goldie Hawn explained that her early career as a dancer came in handy for her starring role as a bawdy dance hall girl in the period western comedy. Hawn's big break came in 1968 when she became a regular cast member in *Rowan & Martin's Laugh-In*. In 1969, she won an Academy Award and a Golden Globe for her supporting role in the film *Cactus Flower*.

RIGHT

Actor Hal Holbrook was cast in the starring role in the 1977 television adaptation of Thornton Wilder's *Our Town*, considered to be one of the best productions of the well-known play. Holbrook made his career playing Mark Twain, performing his one-man stage act starting in 1955 and perfecting it with *Mark Twain Tonight,* which received numerous awards, notably a 1966 Tony for Best Lead Actor in a Play.

LEFT
Semi-Tough was the first book written by Fort Worth native Dan Jenkins. Five years after it was published in 1972, it was released as a feature film. I was an emcee at the film's Fort Worth premiere, which featured cheerleaders and a marching band. A graduate of the *Fort Worth Press*, Jenkins wrote for *Sports Illustrated* for more than thirty years and has published more than twenty books.

Next to him was a large, fake but posh plant which Alex called "Arthur." Arthur was treated as a contributor. To this day people mention to me Alex and his plant friend Arthur.

Pressure from management led ten o'clock anchor Ward Andrews to leave in September 1977. The following year news director Lee Elsesser was replaced by Bill Vance, who had worked for LIN Broadcasting previously. The newsroom was a revolving door on steroids.

Longtime anchor Russ Bloxom saw handwriting on the wall and decided he would leave rather than be fired. When a consultant criticized his folded hands as "too angelic," Bloxom decided to take his angelic hands and his body out of the newsroom. Another anchor, Frank Healer, left and moved to West

Texas. John Gross and Frank Glieber, popular sports anchors, split as well. I still chuckle when I remember Glieber's description of Channel 5 news as "the world's oldest wood-burning newsroom."

Bill Vance hired a couple of guys from a small market in Pennsylvania to run the newsroom. One was the assignment editor and the other his assistant. Both were roly-poly, and behind their backs we called them "Bubba One" and "Bubba Two." Their assignment seemed to be to harass the staff, especially the reporters. I quietly observed their modus operandi, which was to pick one reporter at a time and give that person a hard time. When my time came, Bubba One followed me around the newsroom

ABOVE

A Bridge Too Far was Richard Attenborough's third go at directing films. He had a solid acting career that included Golden Globes for his supporting roles in 1967's *The Sand Pebbles* and 1968's *Doctor Doolittle*. Attenborough produced and directed *Gandhi* in 1983, which earned him Oscars for Best Director and Best Picture, as well as Best Director from the Directors Guild of America and the Golden Globes. He served as president of the Royal Academy of Dramatic Art and the British Academy of Film and Television Arts.

ABOVE RIGHT

I traveled to New York to the 1977 press preview of *A Bridge Too Far,* where I interviewed Anthony Hopkins. It was the Welsh actor's second film with director Richard Attenborough. Hopkins began his acting career on the stage and in films in Britain before moving to the US. He received four Oscar nominations, winning Best Actor in 1992 for *The Silence of the Lambs*. He was knighted by Queen Elizabeth in 1993 but still prefers to be called Tony.

ABOVE

In *A Bridge Too Far*, Elliott Gould joined an illustrious ensemble cast that included Anthony Hopkins, Dirk Bogarde, Michael Caine, Sean Connery, Gene Hackman, Laurence Olivier, Robert Redford, and Maximilian Schell. Based on failed Allied attempts to break through German lines during World War II, the film was one of Gould's earliest dramatic film roles. He received an Oscar nomination for his supporting role in *Bob & Carol & Ted & Alice* and was cast in starring roles in three Robert Altman films: *MASH*, *The Long Goodbye*, and *California Split*.

complaining about what I should include in the story. Wherever I went he was one step behind me. I said nothing for a while. Then when I'd had enough I stopped suddenly and turned to him, saying, "There was no video for what you're recommending, and that was not the story. Okay?" Other reporters I observed getting this treatment, especially women, would usually retire to the restroom and have a good cry. I went back to my desk and continued working. He never bothered me again.

Not long after that, at three o'clock in the afternoon when I was on deadline for a five o'clock story, Bill Vance called me into his office, and his opening line was "I can't afford an entertainment reporter."

I was caught completely off guard, but I immediately replied, "But you've got one."

He looked a bit surprised but continued, "I need a cop reporter and a courthouse reporter and a political reporter."

I said, "Bill, let me be a part of your solution rather than your problem. I'll gladly work general assignments and cut back on entertainment reports."

Sid Caesar's role in comedy's pantheon was major. His zany sketch comedy program *The Show of Shows* (with the wonderful Imogene Coca, among other stars) dominated 1950s television and inspired generations of comedians. The show's writers included Mel Brooks, Neil Simon, and Carl Reiner, who also often appeared onstage. Caesar was a two-time Emmy award winner who occasionally took supporting film roles, as he did in Alan Arkin's *Fire Sale*.

ABOVE
Actor Alan Arkin began his film
directing career in 1971 with the
black comedy *Little Murders,* which
he also starred in. He directed and
starred in the comedy *Fire Sale,*
which he promoted on *Dateline* in
1977. Nominated twice for Best
Actor Oscars, Arkin won a Golden
Globe in 1966 for this starring role
in *The Russians Are Coming,*
The Russians Are Coming.

He obviously had thought ahead of time what he wanted to say to me, and he rattled on, repeating what he needed. In his scenario I was supposed to say, "Well Bill, when do you want me to leave?" I was getting fidgety by the moment. I had an editor waiting for my five o'clock report. Finally I started inching toward the door, saying, "Bill, I have thirty years of blood, sweat, tears, and toil with this company and I ain't leaving." As I approached the door I turned back, and in a carefully modulated voice with no emotion I said, "And I'll be here long after you choose to leave." Exit Bobbie.

When I returned to my desk I couldn't believe I said that, but I wasn't taking back any of it. If Vance wants to get rid of me, he will have to fire me!

TEN

Drafted

The return address on the envelope read "Department of Defense." The letter inside was from the Deputy Secretary of Defense, William Clements. It was about a committee called DACOWITS, Defense Advisory Committee on Women in the Services.

OPPOSITE
Me on my first ride in
an M-48 Patton tank.

I wasn't sure what they wanted from me. I let my husband read it, and Phil said, "Honey, you've been drafted." This was an invitation to serve as a member of the committee.

I called two women who had served previously, and they both said, "By all means accept. It will be a once-in-a-lifetime experience." I signed on and served a three-year term, from 1975 through 1977. It required me to attend four meetings a year in Washington, DC. Some meetings were field trips to camps and military facilities.

The committee consisted of military women and civilian women from all over the country. One of the women I served with was Sandra Day O'Connor, a judge from Arizona who in 1981 became the first woman to serve as a Justice of the Supreme Court.

It was an extremely important time to serve on the committee, because the big issue was admitting women to the service academies.

We made one trip to the Naval Academy before the women arrived and another trip there after the women were admitted. I remember at one luncheon with the cadets I asked the men what they thought about women being admitted to the academy. A senior said it didn't bother him. He thought it was okay for women to be admitted. An underclassman didn't like it at all. When I asked him why, he said, "Because these women have top grades and ratings and they're going to mess up the curve."

I said, "You'll be fine, but I guess you'll have to work a little harder, won't you?"

LEFT
I attended an army press briefing
at Fort Hood in Killeen, Texas.

LEFT
Future Supreme Court justice Sandra Day O'Connor served
on the DACOWITS committee with me in 1975.

ABOVE
Admitting women to military service academies was the main
issue during my three years on the DACOWITS committee.

ABOVE
DACOWITS committee members toured US military bases and talked to female military personnel as part of our orientation.

In a hangar at Andrews Air Force Base in the DC area, I observed two Air Force women struggling with a piece of heavy equipment. I asked them how they liked the Air Force. They both said they liked being in the Air Force, but they thought they would have desk jobs. One said she was going to try to get training for something more suitable for her. The other one said she would not reenlist.

A briefing we had at Camp Lejeune Marine Base in South Carolina was to explain to the committee a recent policy of retiring some officers rather than promoting them to a higher rank. A Marine general who met the description of a tall, lean, fighting machine conducted the briefing with charts and visuals. At the end he asked for questions.

LEFT
A female Naval midshipman
receives instruction in handling
a .30 caliber M1 rifle.

No one spoke. I realized that since I was the only media person on the committee, they were waiting for me to start the questions. I stood and said, "How is this a good use of taxpayer money, when many thousands, maybe millions of dollars have been spent training these officers—and now you're getting rid of them?" The two Marine officers seated on either side of me visibly slouched down in their seats as if to disclaim any connections to me. At a coffee break following the briefing, a Marine officer approached and said, "What *do* you do for a living?"

By the time my three-year term on the DACOWITS Committee ended, I realized that I had had a crash course in how Washington and the government work. I learned how addictive the power of politics could be. We had Pentagon and White House briefings. We got to know women who had spent many years in the service who described the rewards and struggles of their careers. My increased appreciation and respect for these women continue to this day and have influenced me both personally and professionally. Thank you, DACOWITS.

OPPOSITE
Women were granted
permanent status in the
military with benefits
starting in 1948 but were
not admitted to the service
academies until 1976.

OPPOSITE
At US Naval Academy graduation ceremonies, Katherine Engleman receives congratulations from the academy's superintendent, Admiral William P. Lawrence.

ABOVE
The US Military Academy at West Point's 1980 class was the first graduating class to include female cadets.

ELEVEN

Surviving the Suits

Stars occasionally came to Dallas-Fort Worth promoting their movies, but the press tours yielded most of the content of my programs. After seventeen years of interviewing stars, I was beginning to see some of them second and third times around.

OPPOSITE
I interviewed Olivia de Havilland in Los Angeles on Universal's set of *Airport 77,* where de Havilland had just come out of the water after filming the ocean crash landing scene.

In addition to the daily entertainment segment in the 5 p.m. news, I was doing a thirty-minute special once a month. I used longer segments of the celebrity interviews I did for the daily five-minute segments.

I first met Olivia de Havilland and Bette Davis in 1964, when they came to Dallas to promote *Hush . . . Hush, Sweet Charlotte*. Photographer Bob Welch and I arrived early at the Statler-Hilton Hotel to set up. There never was a harder-working, more dedicated photographer than Bob Welch. When our stars arrived, they entered side-by-side, Bette Davis in an attractive dress no doubt from a high-end store. Miss de Havilland was wearing a two-piece designer suit that had to be Chanel. Miss de Havilland was bright and cheerful and said, "We hear you are a very good interviewer." With that she excused herself and went to the end of the large meeting room to greet the photographer. Bette Davis cut to the chase. In a morning voice she said, "Is there any coffee?" While a hotel representative disappeared to fetch coffee, Miss Davis and I sat down. She lit up a cigarette and started telling me that she learned how to do TV interviews from Jack Paar. When coffee arrived she had cup in one hand and cigarette in the other, waving both to accent what she was talking about.

Every so often I'd glance toward the end of the room to see Miss de Havilland and Bob Welch rearranging the setting. Three chairs were moved aside and a settee was moved in. A planter stand was positioned behind the settee. Lights were reset and checked. That being finished, Miss de Havilland came back and stood in front of Miss Davis and me. In a teasing voice she said to Miss Davis, "Bette, while you have been seated here with your coffee chatting with our hostess, I have been working with the cameraman arranging the set. All we need now is for you to check it and see what you think."

LEFT
The 1964 thriller *Hush . . . Hush, Sweet Charlotte* starred two Academy Award-winning actresses, Olivia de Havilland and Bette Davis (left to right). The actresses' fine acting performances helped to elevate and legitimize the horror film. *Hush . . . Hush* received seven Oscar nominations.

With that, Bette Davis, cup in one hand and cigarette in the other, looked up and said, "Olivia dahling, in all the years I've been working before cameras I have used the same makeup and (patting each cheek as she continued) nothing helps it and nothing hurts it." That said, she got up and walked toward the set. Olivia sat in the middle of the settee. I waited for Bette to choose which side she preferred, and I ended up to the left of Olivia. The interview went well. They obviously had worked out what they wanted to say about the movie. My job was to be sure they got equal time.

Later that day, when our lab developed the film, I went to the newsroom to look at the interview. The moment I saw it, I let out a whoop of laughter. There was Olivia in the middle, looking beautiful and younger than springtime, while Bette Davis and I, the bookends, looked like Godzilla!

Those memories were flashing through my mind in 1977, on the back lot of Universal Studios. I was there to interview Olivia de Havilland and Jack Lemmon, who had been shooting scenes for *Airport 77*. When they came to our waiting area, they were dripping wet. The scene they were filming was when the airplane crashes into the ocean. We immediately thought, "Oh swell. We'll have to wait an hour while they get into dry clothes, hair and makeup." But lo and behold, Olivia de Havilland returned first, wearing a terry robe with her wet hair wrapped in a towel and pink tulle. She did take time for makeup. It was as if Melanie from *Gone with the Wind* had reappeared.

Bette Davis and I met again in Dallas a few years after *Hush . . . Hush, Sweet Charlotte*. While we were setting up she held a press

RIGHT
In 1977, I interviewed Woody Allen for *Annie Hall*, Allen's seventh time to direct a feature film. *Annie Hall* hit the Oscar jackpot with wins for Best Picture, Best Director, Best Actress, and Best Original Screenplay.

conference at the other end of the large room. When it was time to do our TV interview, the still photographers all moved to where we were. Miss Davis sat down and eyed the crowd of flashbulbs in front of us. I quietly said to her that our microphones would pick up the clicking noise of the cameras. With that Miss Davis said to the photographers, "All right. You can have one minute and then you must leave." She saw one guy with an extra-long lens. She pointed to him, "You there with the long lens. No nostril shots." She then turned to me and said, "I don't know why editors always want to take the most unflattering shots. Nostril shots should be forbidden." Ever since then, when I want to tell a photographer to keep a head and shoulder shot, I quote Bette Davis. "No nostril shots, please."

My first interview with Woody Allen was in 1977 for *Annie Hall*. He was curled up at one end of a small sofa. He looked so ill at ease. It wasn't until I asked him which comedian he looked up to when he was doing standup that he relaxed and started talking about Bob Hope. When I admitted knowing Bob and also being a Bob Hope fan, he opened up. He said that seeing Bob Hope movies is what inspired him to be a comedian. He admitted to imitating Hope's humor.

I said, "Have you ever met Bob Hope?"

He said, "Oh, no." It was as if Hope would be out of reach for him. The next time I interviewed Bob I asked him if he knew that Woody Allen was a big fan of his work. Bob said that he had been told that, but he had never met Woody. I think Bob was surprised that Woody was such a fan and admirer.

ABOVE

Veteran lyricist Sammy Cahn brought his one-man show *Words and Music* to the Venetian Room in Dallas in 1978. *Words* had had a nine-month run on Broadway, featuring Cahn playing the piano and singing his hit songs, interspersed with stories about his life going back to Tin Pan Alley days. Over his long career, Cahn wrote hundreds of songs, four of which received Academy Awards, including "Three Coins in the Fountain," "All the Way," "High Hopes," and "Call Me Irresponsible."

ABOVE RIGHT

I joined celebrated Irish singer and actor Richard Harris backstage opening night at the Venetian Room. The first show went well until Harris got to "MacArthur Park," a signature song linked to him ever since he had a hit with it in 1968. Harris stumbled haltingly through the song, clutching tightly the lyric sheet on the music stand. After managing to get through to the end of the song, he apologized to the audience. During his interview with me the next day when I teased him about the epic blunder, he blithely blew it off, blaming lack of time to prepare and promising "it's all settled now."

ABOVE

Mel Brooks played a pivotal role in Gene Wilder's rocket to stardom. In his first major film role, Wilder was nominated for an Academy Award for his role in Brooks's farce *The Producers. Blazing Saddles* and *Young Frankenstein* followed, bringing both men phenomenal success. Wilder then teamed up with comedian Richard Pryor in four blockbuster comedies. Wilder started writing and directing his own films, the second of which was *The World's Greatest Lover*, a spoof of silent films and their icon Rudolph Valentino. Wilder talked to me in 1977 about the film and the challenges of simultaneously wearing the hats of writer, producer, director, and star.

ABOVE

I traveled to Los Angeles to interview comedians Jay Leno and Fran Drescher for *American Hot Wax*, one of Leno's first films and Drescher's second. In spite of tepid critical response, the movie helped launch the careers of the two budding comedians. Leno was the Emmy award-winning host of *The Tonight Show* for more than twenty years. Drescher is best known for her starring role in the hit TV sitcom *The Nanny*.

ABOVE RIGHT

At the beginning of his much-heralded movie career, actor William Holden worked with director Billy Wilder in a series of films that became Hollywood classics: *Sunset Boulevard*, *Sabrina*, and *Stalag 17,* for which Holden won an Academy Award for Best Supporting Actor. Holden's final collaboration with Wilder was the French/German production *Fedora*. I caught up with Holden in Los Angeles in 1978 to talk about the film, as well as his recent Oscar-nominated leading role in *Network*.

ABOVE

I interviewed Brian De Palma to talk about *The Fury*, the follow-up to his first hit film *Carrie*. Considered one of the leading New Hollywood directors, De Palma relied on multiple high-speed movie cameras to capture some of the *The Fury's* most dramatic scenes.

LEFT
When I interviewed director Martin Ritt in Chicago for *Norma Rae* in 1979, he was already acknowledged as a major Hollywood director with screen credits that included *The Long, Hot Summer*; *Hud*; *The Spy Who Came in from the Cold*; and *The Great White Hope*. Ritt's well-documented record as a social activist was perfectly suited for *Norma Rae*. The film resulted in Oscar, Golden Globe, and Cannes Film Festival wins for its star Sally Field.

BELOW
Claude Akins costarred with Shirley Jones in *Yesterday's Child*. During his interview with me to promote the TV movie he talked about his long career as a character actor in television series such as *My Friend Flicka*, *Gunsmoke*, *The Restless Gun*, *Wagon Train*, *The Rifleman*, *Bonanza*, and *Dick Powell's Zane Grey Theatre*. Still in his future was his best-known TV role of Sheriff Lobo in *B.J. and the Bear*.

ABOVE
After appearing in Brian de Palma's *Carrie*, Amy Irving was cast in the leading role of his thriller *The Fury*. It was Irving's second feature film. At the beginning of her career, Irving appeared in episodic television shows such as *Happy Days* and *Police Woman*, and played Juliet in the Los Angeles Free Shakespeare Theatre's 1975 production of *Romeo and Juliet*. She received an Oscar nomination for her supporting role in Barbra Streisand's directorial debut *Yentl*.

ABOVE

The film *Luna* came at a critical point in Jill Clayburgh's career—she had just received an Academy Award nomination for Best Actress for *An Unmarried Woman*. During her interview with me in New York, Clayburgh talked about working in Italy with director Bernardo Bertolucci, whose previous film release was his epic *1900*. After starring roles in two Broadway musicals, Clayburgh was introduced to film audiences in *Gable and Lombard*, *Silver Streak*, and *Semi-Tough*.

ABOVE RIGHT

I interviewed comedian Redd Foxx in Los Angeles in 1980 just before the TV debut of *Sanford*, a sequel to the hit black sitcom *Sanford and Son*. Everyone from the original cast, except one, returned for the second series. The original program was in the top ten for five of its six seasons but was cancelled when Foxx left to star in his own variety show, *The Redd Foxx Show*. The name of Foxx's character, Fred G. Sanford, was the real-life name of his father and brother.

ABOVE

After a four-year run in the popular musical sitcom *The Partridge Family*, in 1977 Shirley Jones took the lead role in the TV drama *Yesterday's Child*. I interviewed her in Los Angeles about the film and her life after Partridge. It was Shirley Jones's notable singing ability that got her noticed in the 1950s by Richard Rodgers and Oscar Hammerstein, who cast her in the film adaptations of their musicals *Oklahoma!*, *Carousel*, and *The Music Man*. In 1960, Jones won an Academy Award for her dramatic supporting role in *Elmer Gantry*.

ABOVE LEFT

My 1978 interview with Peter Sellers for *The Revenge of the Pink Panther* was my last with the British actor, who died two years later. Prior to *The Pink Panther*, Sellers had a supporting role in Stanley Kubrick's *Lolita,* which resulted in a Golden Globe nomination. His starring role in Kubrick's next film *Dr. Strangelove* included playing three characters, a feat that was recognized with an Academy Award nomination. He also starred in the wacky comedy *What's New Pussycat?*, Woody Allen's first produced screenplay.

ABOVE

The Revenge of the Pink Panther was the fifth *Panther* in the series that was written, produced, and directed by Blake Edwards. I was invited to Hawaii to attend the press previews for the 1978 film. The *Panther* franchise began in 1963, quickly establishing the box office power of Edwards and his star Peter Sellers. Edwards, who created the *Peter Gunn* TV series, found success writing and directing comedy and drama for both the large and small screens, directing such hits as *Operation Petticoat*, *Breakfast at Tiffany's*, *Days of Wine and Roses*, and *The Great Race*.

ABOVE

The Revenge of the Pink Panther was Dyan Cannon's first film with Peter Sellers and Blake Edwards. Her acting talents were recognized by Academy Award and Golden Globe nominations for her supporting role in 1969's *Bob & Carol & Ted & Alice*. She was nominated again for a Golden Globe for her starring role in 1971's *Such Good Friends*. Her supporting role in *Heaven Can Wait* brought her another set of Golden Globe and Oscar nominations.

RIGHT

I interviewed actress Sally Kellerman about working with Jodie Foster in *Foxes,* which was Adrian Lyne's feature film directorial debut in 1980. While pursuing a singing career, Kellerman started acting in television series in the 1960s, notably *Dobie Gillis, Bachelor Father, My Three Sons, Twilight Zone, Outer Limits,* and *Star Trek.* Her breakthrough role in film was as Hot Lips Houlihan in Robert Altman's *MASH,* which earned her Academy Award and Golden Globe nominations. The offbeat actress worked with Altman again on *Brewster McCloud* and had leading roles in *Last of the Red Hot Lovers* and *Welcome to L.A.*

RIGHT

I was one of seventy journalists invited to a three-day press preview in Flagstaff, Arizona, for the 1979 disaster film *Meteor.* A special reception was held at the nearby Meteor Crater, one of the largest and best-preserved meteor impact sites in the world. When I interviewed actor Sean Connery in Flagstaff, he told me he was happy with the success of the James Bond movies, but welcomed other film roles like *Meteor.* Connery demonstrated his versatile acting skills in films such as *Marnie, Murder on the Orient Express, Robin and Marian,* and *A Bridge Too Far.*

RIGHT

Natalie Wood starred with Sean Connery in *Meteor,* which turned out to be one of her last motion pictures before her death in 1983. The high-profile Hollywood star got her first Oscar nomination in 1955 for her supporting role in *Rebel Without a Cause* and was awarded a Golden Globe for Best New Star. She was nominated again for an Academy Award in 1961 for *Splendor in the Grass.* Her leading roles in *West Side Story* and *Gypsy* helped to make those films commercial successes. *Love with the Proper Stranger* resulted in her third Oscar nomination. She won the Golden Globe for Best Actress in 1980 for her starring role in the TV miniseries *From Here to Eternity.*

ABOVE

At a party after the first performance of "An Evening with Pat Boone" at Casa Mañana in 1979, I presented Boone with a photo poster commemorating his early days on Channel 5. After leaving WBAP-TV in 1955, he became one of the biggest-selling recording artists of his era and starred in twelve motion pictures.

Gregory Peck was another actor I interviewed a number of times. I found him to be always a gentleman and always cooperative. When he did interviews for *The Old Gringo* in 1989, I happened to see the young woman ahead of me interviewing him. She admitted she was new at press tours, but in closing the interview, she said, "May I kiss you?" Peck was taken aback but he mumbled, "If you like," and she leaned over and gave him a big smack on the lips. I followed her, and I kidded Peck about taking cooperation to a new level. I don't recall ever seeing that reporter on another press tour.

My first interview with Gregory Peck was in 1962 for *To Kill a Mockingbird*. When I asked him if the role of Atticus was difficult to play, he said, "Not at all. I was playing my father."

A few years later Peck came to Fort Worth and Dallas for a nonprofit organization, and I spent an entire day with him. On the ride from one place to another we talked about one of my all-time favorite movies, *Roman Holiday*. Peck spoke fondly of Audrey Hepburn. He said he knew she would emerge from that film a big star, and he campaigned for her to have equal billing. He said it was through *Roman Holiday* that he met his wife.

At the time Peck had gone through a divorce and was "very single." Before filming *Roman Holiday* in Rome, he was in Paris. An interview was set up with a newspaper reporter who turned out to be a very attractive young French woman named Veronique. The interview went longer than usual. Six months later, when he finished *Roman Holiday*, Peck went back to Paris, called Veronique, and invited her to lunch. While talking with her on the phone and paying her compliments, he learned later that their entire conversation was on loudspeaker throughout the newsroom. That was the beginning of their romance. Their marriage on New Year's Day 1956 lasted almost fifty years, until Peck's death in 2003.

In 1976 Universal Pictures had a press tour for *MacArthur*, based on the famous general of World War II and Korea. We were bussed to Camp Pendleton in California to see Gregory Peck on location. We all had doubts about how the handsome Gregory Peck was going to play the tough-looking, weathered soldier. When Peck stepped out from his trailer to meet our group, we were astonished to see how much he looked like Douglas MacArthur. I actually forgot it was Gregory Peck on the screen. He *was* General MacArthur.

Back at KXAS-TV, a fresh-faced, ambitious young reporter named Scott Pelley joined the newsroom staff in 1978. A college dropout, he was only twenty-one years old, but stood out because he was already a good reporter and took his job very seriously. Another promising reporter who joined the staff was Karen Parfitt (Hughes). She was a crackerjack KXAS reporter for seven years before serving in George W. Bush's White House.

Program Director Bob Gould retired in 1979. The new PD would be Charlie Rose, who had met our station manager Blake Byrne when Charlie was doing a radio talk show in Chicago. Both were Duke University graduates. Charlie wanted to do a TV talk

ABOVE
Gregory Peck was one of my favorite stars to interview. I spent an entire day with him in 1965 when he was in Fort Worth and Dallas on behalf of a nonprofit organization.

OPPOSITE AND BELOW
In 1976, the press corps was invited to visit the filming of *MacArthur* at Camp Pendleton in California. Gregory Peck is in costume. In the photo below I'm with the group on the left.

show along the lines of Phil Donahue, but Byrne said the only way he could justify that would be if Rose took the program director job as well.

Soon after Charlie Rose arrived at KXAS-TV he asked me to come to his office. After pleasantries were exchanged, Charlie got to the purpose of the meeting. He wanted me to use my contacts to help him get guests for his new talk show. In effect, I would help him book his show. I let him know straight away that I had my hands full keeping up with my own shows, much less taking on any new assignments. He wasn't happy, but he didn't pursue it any further.

Charlie Rose had some success with his talk show, but he was difficult. The crew disliked him, and with good reason. One time Charlie made a mistake on air, and as soon as they went to commercials, in front of a studio audience Charlie blamed the mistake on one of the production crew and proceeded to chew him out. The rest of the crew was furious. Later that day I happened to pass the production office and saw the berated crew guy with his head down on the desk. He was so upset and afraid Charlie might get him fired. I went to the young man and said, "Most people in this business are good, but every once in a while you meet the other kind. Don't let S.O.B.s ruin your life. Consider the source and move on."

Later some of the production crew said to me, "We don't know what you told him, but he's okay now. Thanks."

Charlie Rose left KXAS-TV in 1981 and eventually ended up in New York. He developed into an excellent interviewer whose work has been recognized with Emmy and Peabody awards. While he didn't win any popularity polls from fellow workers at KXAS, there were no reports of sexual harassment. That was to come many years later.

In 1979 another big change. We were no longer the *Texas News*. We were *Action News!* This was supposed to give us a new, more aggressive image and, management hoped, higher ratings.

Another big shakeup came in 1980. Chip Moody left to go to Channel 4, then the local CBS affiliate. At that time nobody was under contract. To this day I have never signed a contract with the station. Today most anchors would have a clause in the contract stating that if the anchor leaves KXAS-TV, he or she cannot go to work for another station in the market for a specified amount of time—usually six months.

Chip was unhappy with the new management. Channel 4 KDFW-TV offered him an anchor position and more money. KXAS-TV management kept putting off a counteroffer. Finally KDFW-TV set a deadline. When the deadline came and KXAS-TV still had no counteroffer, Chip Moody moved to Channel 4.

Scott Pelley jumped ship in 1982 to join Channel 8, which was then number one in ratings. In 1989 he was hired by CBS in New York. A multiple Peabody, Emmy, and du Pont award-winning journalist, he has been one of *60 Minutes*'s mainstay correspondents and was, for six years, the lead anchor and managing editor of the *CBS Evening News*.

During this time I didn't know where I stood with Bill Vance. My reputation as the only fulltime entertainment reporter and critic in the market was acknowledged locally and by film studios. One day Vance signaled for me to come into his office. He reached down, opened a desk drawer, and took out a paper. He covered the top third and said, "Read the rest of the page." It was a report from Magid, our consultants. The more I read, the more I couldn't believe it. This was a valentine. Magid had checked a five o'clock newscast where I reviewed *American Gigolo*, a movie starring Richard Gere. I took issue with one full shot of Gere nude. Admittedly, Gere was cast as a male prostitute, but the nude shot seemed gratuitous and insulting to

ABOVE
Charlie Rose's proof sheet for his 1979 KXAS head shot. Rose accepted the job of program director at KXAS after management agreed that he could also have his own talk show.

ABOVE
Charlie Rose debuted his first television
talk show in 1979 at the Channel 5 studios.

ABOVE RIGHT
Rose patterned *The Charlie Rose Show*
after Phil Donahue's popular topical talk
show, which had a live audience that
participated in on-air discussions.

RIGHT
Rose interviewed rival TV anchors, WFAA's
Tracy Rowlett (left) and KXAS's Chip Moody
(right). Despite his talent, Rose ruffled
feathers and was gone in two years.

ABOVE
(Left to right) Chief Meteorologist
Harold Taft, anchor Chip Moody, and
Sportscaster Jim Brinson.

OPPOSITE
The 1979 KXAS-TV Action News Team: back row (left to right): Scott Pelley, Bill Vance,
Ben Pate, Louis Zapata, Bob Welch, Dave Dosker, Carmen Vasquez. Second row from back,
left to right: Cary Simms, Mitch Wilson, Tom McDonald, Mike Snyder, Mike Lane, Renee Watkins,
Dru Williams, (unknown), Nate Tarpley. Third row from back (left to right): Dick Smith,
Mark Young, Bobbie Wygant, David Finfrock, Paula Drew, Andie Hayes, Ed Martelle, (unknown),
Tyrone Turner, Joe Johnson. Fourth row from back (left to right): (unknown), (unknown).
Fifth row from back (left to right): Dick McElvany, Martha Pingel, Bill Hix, Lee Elsesser,
Jack Brown, Doug Adams. Sixth row from back (left to right): Harold Taft, Brad Wright,
Jane Jayroe, Jim Brinson. Sitting in front row (left to right): Pam Moore, Dave Layman.

ABOVE LEFT
Texas News was cancelled and replaced with *Action News!* in 1979.

ABOVE
Dave Layman and Jane Jayroe, Miss America 1967, were named the new lead anchors at KXAS in 1980.

the audience. I thought it cheapened the film. After the review the anchors joined me in a brief discussion. The Magid review said that this was the best part of the newscast. They had only praise for me and my work. When I finished reading it over Vance's shoulder, I said, "That's very nice. Thank you for showing it to me. I'd like to have a copy if I may." He said, "Yeah." But I never saw a copy. I was puzzled as to why he showed it to me. I concluded it was his way of saying, "You've been saved by Magid!" If I were reviewing this film today, I probably wouldn't have the same reaction to the nude shot, but in 1980 it was the talk of *American Gigolo,* and I wasn't the only critic who had the same opinion about it.

With Chip Moody gone, Bill Vance brought in Dave Layman, an anchor he had worked with in Rhode Island. Layman thought he was Superman. He wanted to be in the field to cover the top story of the day, then rush back to the anchor desk and say, "Look what I have for you tonight." Maybe in a small market that would work, but it doesn't work in a dual-city market like Fort Worth-Dallas. Layman would work on a story, come rushing back to the station, write the story, and dash to the anchor desk with hair and tie blowing in the wind. His delivery of the rest of the news wasn't always smooth. Dave Layman was the extreme opposite of Chip Moody, who always had it together. I knew we were in trouble when a neighbor stopped me one day and said, "Where did Channel 5 get that new anchor? Off a used-car lot?"

To coanchor with Dave Layman, management brought in Jane Jayroe. She was Miss America in 1967. Jane had worked for a TV station in Oklahoma. She took her work seriously and was a lovely person. Layman was let go in 1982. Jane Jayroe left in 1984 and went back to Oklahoma.

My boss Bill Vance left me alone to do my work until one afternoon when I was leaving

The Dallas Morning News

TV CHANNELS
Week of March 8, 1981

Sissy Spacek

Dustin Hoffman

Dolly Parton

Bobbie Wygant: backlighting the stars

ED BARK / TV-Radio

Bobbie Wygant wants her stars to shine

WHETHER suffering at the little hands of Ricky Schroder or showing Dustin Hoffman a genuinely good time, venerable Bobbie Wygant is unfailingly buoyant and undeniably professional.

Her monthly *Entertainment and the Arts* specials are Channel 5's avenue to the stars. It's obvious she primps and prepares for each celebrity. In return, she expects more than just the time of day from notables promoting their latest activities.

"A lot of stars get very uptight about interviews," Ms. Wygant said in a recent interview. "They just are in a nervous tizzy. So many of your television stars are people who have very little background in the business. And there's nobody trying to help them. It's such a mill and a factory. It's not like the old studio days where they actually learned how to give good interviews. They learned how to dress for a picture session. Not only did they learn, but they had to pass inspection, as it were. Now I see actors and actresses coming in and schlepping around, looking like they just came in from washing the car. In the old days that would never have happened."

FOR MS. WYGANT, the "old days" date to 1960, when she graduated from Purdue University and debuted on Channel 5 with a program called *Dateline*. It was a "basic local interview show" that ran for 14 years until Linn Broadcasting bought Channel 5 in 1974.

"I used to say, 'If it isn't illegal or immoral, I'll put it on,'" Ms. Wygant recalled.

Her next assignment was a 5 p.m. "magazine format" program co-hosted by Chip Moody. In 1977, the station switched to "hard news" at 5 p.m. and Ms. Wygant found herself in limbo for awhile. News director Bill Vance wasn't sure he could afford a full-time "entertainment and the arts person," she said. Eventually, Channel 5 management decided it couldn't afford to lose her. And so she endures as the only Dallas-Fort Worth television performer with a regularly scheduled half hour celebrity showcase.

"As they say in television, 'working quick and dirty,' I think I do a good job," Ms. Wygant said.

"Quick and dirty" means an allotment of about 10 minutes per star. When she travels to New York or Los Angeles, Ms. Wygant often is one of 30 reporters penciled in for a brief interview. The time constraints

are relaxed a bit when celebrities come to Channel 5's Fort Worth studios.

"I'LL TRY to find some angle so they're not just sitting there doing the commercial to get people to go see the picture," Ms. Wygant said. "I try never to be in awe of them because I think the minute they sense that, it does something to the professional relationship. I don't want to sit there like some little teenybopper and say, 'Ooh, I just love you.' It's not my nature to do that.

"I read people pretty well," she added, noting her "double major" in psychology at Purdue. "I don't come at them as if they were on the witness stand and I'm a prosecuting attorney. I find giving them a little gentle jab sometimes works just as well, if not better. I've seen other interviewers just really strike out, and their subjects just drop the curtain and clam up."

She had a memorable conversation with Hoffman after opening the interview with a simple, disarming, slightly naughty question. Ms. Wygant noted the somewhat reclusive actor was doing hundreds of interviews for the film, *Kramer Vs. Kramer*, after refusing to tour the country on behalf of the many other movies he's made since *The Graduate*.

"Why are you working your buns off?" she asked him.

Hoffman seemed genuinely charmed by the question and loosened up immediately. He offered a humorous discourse on his "buns" and then gave long, thoughtful answers to Ms. Wygant's other concise questions.

After the formal session ended, Hoffman said, "She's alright. That was a great interview. Who's your sponsor, Hot Cross Buns?"

IT'S ALL on tape, as is a somewhat less scintillating interview with Schroder, the child star, who recently visited Dallas to promote *The Earthling*. Virtually all of his answers were quick one-liners, but the indefatigable Ms. Wygant continued to pump questions, never pausing, using every second of the time allotted to her. A less prepared interviewer might have either given up or been reduced to a stammering mess. Sometimes grown-up stars can be a problem, too. Ms. Wygant said her most disappointing interview was with Charlton Heston, who was supposed to be touting the movie, *Will Penny*.

"His answers were 'Well . . . uh . . . er,' and he just ate up time with that," she recalled. "I was livid with him because I knew I was giving him good stuff and he wasn't cooperating. Later I found out he was unhappy because it was a beautiful day and he wanted to play tennis."

Ms. Wygant said she had better luck in subsequent interviews with Heston, who has been "dynamite" since fizzling.

WHILE PROMOTING *9 to 5*, Jane Fonda got a bit miffed when Ms. Wygant asked her what kind of president Ronald Reagan would be.

"When the interview was finished, Jane said, 'I bet you didn't ask Dolly Parton that.'"

"I sensed a little edge to her voice," Ms. Wygant said. "She said nobody thinks she has a sense of humor because they always ask her the serious and news-related questions.'

"'But Jane, you speak out on these things,'" Ms. Wygant said she told the Oscar-winning actress. "'Even if people don't ask you, you're vocal with your opinions and you have taken stands. You're a natural person to ask questions like that.'

"I think sometimes it isn't what someone says, but how they say it," she said. "I like animation. And of course, you want them to directly answer the question. You know there are some people who you ask the time and they tell you how to build a watch. I want something people will perk up their ears to listen to, but I don't like people who work at being provocative. The good people are the ones who make it seem spontaneous, no matter how many interviews they've done."

Ms. Wygant says she won't ask questions that invade a celebrity's privacy. Otherwise, though, she'd like them to tell it all in an entertaining manner. In her case, there is one non-answerable question. Her biography includes information on her husband (former Channel 5 executive Philip Wygant), their homes and a cabin cruiser named "Good Grief. There's no birthdate, though.

"If you were to print my age, there would be people who would immediately hold that against me,'" Ms. Wygant explained. "As long as we're in a youth-oriented society, middle-aged men and women should forget about their age. It doesn't serve me well to give mine, so I finally said, 'The hell with it.'"

26 TV CHANNELS Week of March 8, 1981 **The Dallas Morning News**

ABOVE
I made the cover of the *Dallas Morning News TV Channels* in March 1981. The article by *Dallas Morning News*'s TV-Radio critic Ed Bark profiled my career and included some of my favorite inside stories about celebrities.

the station to go to the airport. I was flying to New York for a press premiere of *Superman* with Christopher Reeve interviews. As I passed Vance's door, car keys in hand, he called out, "Bobbie, Bobbie." I came back as he continued, "You'll have to call off the trip. I need you here to cover the Van Cliburn Competition."

I said, "Bill, we have that taken care of for Saturday and I'll be back Sunday in time to cover the finals." He insisted that I must cancel the trip and stay in town. I raised my voice saying, "Another newsroom screw up!" And I

stormed out of his office. It's the only time I let my anger show. I went back to my desk, slammed my bag down, picked up the phone, and called my husband to say, "I'm not going to New York. I'm on my way home." Later I was told the entire newsroom came to a halt. No one had ever seen me ruffled, much less angry. It seems the reason Vance cancelled my trip was that the station manager had become a board member of the Van Cliburn International Piano Competition and he told Vance to have the A-team cover the finals that weekend. Vance was afraid that having

ABOVE
For a few brief moments, I lived my lifelong dream to be a symphony conductor, thanks to the Fort Worth Symphony and its conductor John Giordano, who gave me a hug at the finale.

a reporter work it Saturday with me covering the finals on Sunday would not look like the A-team. I was furious that he didn't tell me to cancel the trip until I was on my way. In another five seconds I would have been on the way to the airport. I wondered later if he hadn't stopped me going out the door, would he have had me dragged off the plane before takeoff?

After several weeks of steering clear of each other I had to go in and talk with Vance about another matter. I was very businesslike, but before I left I said, "Bill, I'm not apologizing for what I said, but I do apologize for losing my temper."

He looked up and half smiling said, "I knew you were pissed."

TWELVE

Working Your Buns Off

By the mid-seventies nearly all of the major studios were participating in press tours to promote their movies. United Artists, Columbia, Warner Bros., 20th Century Fox, Sony, Disney, Paramount, Universal.

OPPOSITE
I hit it off with Dustin Hoffman when I interviewed him for *Kramer vs. Kramer*. The film swept the 1980 Academy Awards, including Hoffman's first win, after he'd been nominated three times before for *The Graduate, Midnight Cowboy,* and *Lenny*.

Many of them had their own local representatives in Dallas or an advertising agency working local and regional press contacts.

Most trips were on weekends. I would get my shows taped for Friday and the weekend, if I had a thirty-minute special that weekend. I'd spend my time on the airplane preparing the interviews I would do in Los Angeles, New York, Toronto, wherever. It was a time of work, work, work, but I thrived on it. I could have been a professional student. Preparing interviews was enjoyable. If only we had had laptops, the internet, and Google in those days! It's probably just as well, because when I do research on the internet there's no stopping place. It goes on and on. I would have had even less sleep.

Occasionally the stars would come to Dallas-Fort Worth. In 1979 Dustin Hoffman came to Dallas for *Kramer vs Kramer*. I started the interview by saying, "On this tour you're doing over 325 interviews. Why are you working your buns off?" Hoffman processed the question as if it were an exercise in improvisation. He laughed and then launched into a monologue about his buns being so large he had to start working them to get them smaller. He loved it—thought it was a good interview. When he won the Oscar for best actor that year it was plain why he wanted to work his buns off.

When *Tootsie* came out in 1982 I again interviewed Dustin Hoffman. In most of the scenes Hoffman portrayed an actress, a role for which he received an Oscar nomination. I started the interview reminding him about our earlier "buns" conversation for *Kramer vs Kramer*. I asked him how his buns were now. Hoffman picked up where he left off, saying

that he had to get his buns in shape to wear the dresses in *Tootsie*. Sydney Pollack, who directed *Tootsie,* said that one of the problems he had with Dustin was that he kept pulling down the girdle. Pollack said he had to keep editing out those shots. I reminded him, "But we do see him grabbing the girdle." Pollack said, "So I gave him one yank!"

Ishtar was one of my most unforgettable interviews. Warren Beatty and Dustin Hoffman together was a combination destined to send Columbia promotion executives to the nearest funny farm. One publicist said he spent his days on the phone with Dustin in one ear and Warren in the other. I remember the day I received a call from a Columbia executive asking my opinion about something Warren Beatty wanted for the press interviews coming up in Los Angeles. Warren wanted to shoot the interviews on

35mm movie film. "How do you think the TV press will react to that?" he said.

I replied, "Where does Warren think we'll run them—at our local movie theaters?"

When the day came to do the interviews in a Westwood hotel meeting room, you would have thought it was a scene from *Gone with the Wind*. There was so much equipment that we had to be taken by the hand and led through a maze of light stands and cable. Behind Dustin and Warren was a window with a three-dimensional background. The distance between the interviewer and the two stars was so far that I wondered if we'd need a megaphone to make ourselves heard. As I sat down for this three-camera shoot, I looked up and saw the operator of my camera peeking around his lens and giving a little wave in my direction. I nearly fainted. It was William "Willie" Fraker, a five-time Academy Award

ABOVE LEFT
Tootsie was the perfect showcase for Dustin Hoffman's versatile acting abilities.

© 1982 Columbia Pictures Industries, Inc. All rights reserved. Courtesy of Columbia Pictures.

ABOVE
Warren Beatty (left) and Dustin Hoffman in *Ishtar.*

© 1982 Columbia Pictures Industries, Inc. All rights reserved. Courtesy of Columbia Pictures.

RIGHT
Shirley MacLaine won an Academy Award and Golden Globe in 1984 for *Terms of Endearment*. She had previously won Golden Globes for 1961's *The Apartment* and 1964's *Irma la Douce*. During her many interviews with me, she always insisted on being lit with a single white light placed low.

FAR RIGHT
My first interview with Meryl Streep was in 1982 for *Sophie's Choice*.

nominee for cinematography. Fraker was famous for one of the chase scenes in *Bullitt* in which he and his camera were strapped to the front of a Mustang going up and down the hills of San Francisco at 100 mph. Willie Fraker was shooting *Ishtar* interviews! When Beatty's preference for 35mm film was turned down, he settled for 16mm film, which was converted to tape for the TV press. Beatty thought film as the source was more flattering than tape. I love this job!

Another time I was interviewing Warren Beatty at the Four Seasons Hotel in Beverly Hills, and Warren stopped the interview because he was hearing sounds from workmen someplace in the hotel. He dispatched a studio representative to tell them to stop the noise. The sound man said it didn't seem to be picking up on the microphones around our necks. But Warren didn't give the okay

to continue until the noise stopped. After a minute or so it started again. With that, Beatty took off his microphone and stormed out of the room. He went directly to the front desk and demanded that the noise be stopped. When he came back, we picked up where we left off. The noise did not return. Don't mess with Warren Beatty.

I once asked Shirley MacLaine when she and her brother Warren Beatty were going to make a movie together. Her reply was, "When Warren can do a scene in less than sixty-five takes."

Meryl Streep received a best supporting actress Oscar nomination for *Kramer vs. Kramer*, but my first meeting with her was in New York in 1982, for *Sophie's Choice*. I thought it was an incredible performance. The day of the interviews Meryl was not feeling well. She was pregnant with her second child and was having a bad case of morning sickness. Nonetheless she was keeping to her interviews with the TV press. She had soda crackers on a table next to her, and between interviews she would go to the adjoining room and lie down for a few minutes.

I started by thanking her for doing the interviews in spite of having morning sickness. Her attitude was "No big deal. This is my job. It's important." And indeed, it only added to the respect everyone had for her performance. In my interview she readily acknowledged she was not producer/director Alan J. Pakula's first choice for the role. When I talked with Pakula, he said he had wanted a Czechoslovakian actress, but the studio insisted on someone Americans would know. Pakula wrote the adaptation of William Styron's novel. He didn't know how Meryl got the carefully guarded script, but Meryl came completely prepared for the audition. Her Polish accent was perfect. She understood the character. Pakula had to give her the role. Streep's portrayal won her the 1982 Academy Award for Best Actress.

In 1981 I got a call from Marianne Mitchell, the Dallas representative for Universal Pictures, to come to Chicago to interview John Belushi. I didn't come back with a quick response. Then I began thinking out loud and started telling Marianne that I did not have good experiences with Belushi. In 1975, at NBC's pre-season press tour in Los Angeles, John Belushi was on the list representing *Saturday Night Live*. My camera operator Billy Glover, promotion director Phil Wygant, and I filmed forty interviews in two days. Talk about work intensive! When Belushi came in, for some reason we did the interview standing. I began the introduction, and Belushi interrupted to say, "You're from Dallas, right?" Then he looked directly into the camera and said, "Dallas, the city that killed my president." I was so shocked, I was speechless. I fumbled around and asked a couple of questions about

LEFT
Comedian John Belushi (right) knew how to unnerve me and made a point to do it in every interview we did, starting in 1975 for *Saturday Night Live* and again in 1980 for *The Blues Brothers*.

Saturday Night Live and then terminated the interview. When he left, the three of us looked at one another still in a state of shock. The 1963 assassination of President Kennedy was still a tender subject to Texans. Needless to say, the interview never made air. NBC was embarrassed by Belushi's actions.

Fast forward to 1980. A call from Marianne Mitchell, Universal's representative in Dallas. "We're inviting you to Chicago to interview the director and stars of our movie, *The Blues Brothers*. You'll talk with John Belushi, Dan Aykroyd, and director John Landis." The interviews were on Sunday, which is always worrisome because that's also a travel home day. The interviews were behind schedule from the beginning. Belushi was taking more breaks than usual. Finally, it was my turn. When I started the first question, Belushi popped up and said, "I remember you. You're from Dallas, the city that killed my president."

John Landis and Dan Aykroyd both screamed "John!" I couldn't believe we were reliving the 1975 incident. Both Aykroyd and Landis were shocked and jumped in to try to smooth things over. Once again that part of the interview never made air.

So when *Continental Divide* came up in 1981, you can readily see why I didn't jump at the opportunity to talk with John Belushi. I told Marianne Mitchell I would attend, but she must tell Universal and John Belushi that if he says "Dallas, the city that killed my president," I would walk. "I'm not taking any more of that," I told her.

When I was escorted to the interview room, the door opened with John Belushi standing in the doorway. He took my hand and in a very contrite voice said, "I promise you. I won't say it."

I said, "I hope not, John, because if you do, I will walk."

As we went to take our seats next to Blair Brown, his leading lady in *Continental Divide*, John had his arm around my shoulder and was saying, "I'll be a good boy."

I said, "It's up to you, John."

When we sat down, Blair Brown said, "What are you two up to?"

I said, "We'll tell you later."

With that the producer said, "Standby and action."

I started the introduction, but Blair said, "I want to know now. What's going on with you two?"

She kept at it and finally John said, "Bobbie doesn't like it when I say, 'Dallas, the city that killed my president.'" He looked at me as if to say, "She made me do it." I just shook my head. You're right. That part never made air.

John Belushi died in 1982. I did a live tribute to him on the noon news, and for the first time ever I told the stories about "Dallas, the city that killed my president." I explained that these stories summed up John Belushi and what he was all about. To John, nothing was sacred. Anything and everything was fair game in his act. Shocking an audience was

RIGHT
John Belushi starred in *Continental Divide* in 1981. He died six months after the film's release.

his method of communication.

A few years later, in 1985, I was doing an interview with John's brother, Jim Belushi, who was in the Tom Hanks movie *The Man with One Red Shoe*. The crew was having a technical problem so Jim and I had a few minutes to talk while the crew took care of business. I told Jim my three experiences with John, and I said that the line never made air until I did a tribute to John when he died. Jim said my summation of John was right. When it came to performing, nothing was sacred to John, not even assassinated presidents.

Back at the TV station, in the '80s the

LEFT
When comedian George Burns was seventy-nine, he replaced his ailing friend Jack Benny in *The Sunshine Boys,* and his career went into overdrive. His supporting role in the 1974 film was awarded an Oscar, and two years later he starred in another hit film, *Oh, God!* I caught up with Burns in Las Vegas in 1984 where he was promoting the third and final installment of the *God* series, *Oh, God! You Devil.* Burns's vaudeville career was launched in 1923 with the Burns and Allen act, costarring his future wife Gracie Allen. The pair went on to appear in feature films and on radio starting in the 1930s and 40s. *The George Burns and Gracie Allen Show* ran on television from 1950 until 1958.

OPPOSITE
British comedian Dudley Moore made an impromptu wardrobe adjustment during his interview with me for *Unfaithfully Yours.* Peter Sellers was originally cast as the lead in the 1984 film, but upon Sellers's death the role went to Moore. Moore spent the early years of his career in England, where he worked as a jazz pianist and composer as well as a comedian in film and television. When he moved to the States, he landed a series of roles in hit films including *Foul Play, 10,* and *Arthur*—the latter resulting in an Oscar nomination and a Golden Globe win. Moore won a second Golden Globe for *Micki & Maude* in 1984.

ratings for KXAS-TV and the NBC network were not good. ABC Network and its Dallas affiliate WFAA-TV were on top. Staff members at KXAS-TV continued to leave, some by choice and others terminated. By 1982 our news ratings at 6 and 10 p.m. had dropped from first to third place.

Blake Byrne, the president and general manager brought in by LIN Broadcasting when the station was sold, left in 1982. Byrne moved up LIN's corporate ladder to become group vice president for LIN.

In 1983, News Director Bill Vance was replaced by Doug Adams, a longtime newsroom employee from the WBAP-TV days. Doug was in charge of our Dallas News Bureau.

A big event for me in 1984 was interviewing Paul McCartney for his movie *Give My Regards to Broad Street.* The song "No More Lonely Nights" won Golden Globe and BAFTA awards, but the majority of critics panned the movie. Being a Beatles fan, my review was, "With Paul McCartney as the star it can't be all bad."

The thing I remember most about the press tour for the film was the security around McCartney. John Lennon had been shot and killed in front of his New York apartment in December 1980. Security for McCartney

ABOVE LEFT

I interviewed actor Leonard Nimoy in 1979 for *Star Trek: The Motion Picture*, the first of eight feature films Nimoy starred in as Spock, the role he made famous in the *Star Trek* television series.

ABOVE

I discovered during my 1979 interview with DeForest Kelley that he had been offered the Spock role in the *Star Trek* television series, but turned it down for the part of Dr. Leonard "Bones" McCoy, which he played in all three seasons of the TV series and in six of the *Star Trek* movies.

ABOVE

James Woods began his Hollywood acting career in 1972, often cast in dark character roles. In 1984, I interviewed him about his starring role in *Against All Odds*, a remake of the film noir classic *Out of the Past*.

ABOVE LEFT

1983's *Two of a Kind* was the second film that starred Olivia Newton-John and John Travolta. Even though the film did disappointing box office, the soundtrack went platinum. The pair was first cast together in *Grease*, the number one film in 1978 and one of the highest-grossing film musicals ever. John Travolta made his name in the TV sitcom *Welcome Back, Kotter* and in the landmark film *Saturday Night Fever*. Four-time Grammy winner Olivia Newton-John's recording career was red hot in the 1960s and 70s and included five number-one Billboard singles, with two platinum and four double-platinum albums.

ABOVE

While starring in the top-ten TV sitcom *Cheers*, Ted Danson also did movies, including 1986's *Just Between Friends*. When I interviewed him about the film, I couldn't resist asking him about the phenomenal success of *Cheers*. During that show's eleven seasons, Danson received two Emmys, with nominations every year the show aired, as well as nine Golden Globe nominations and two wins.

ABOVE

Mary Tyler Moore wanted to expand her horizons after starring in two of television's most beloved sitcoms. In 1980, she won a Golden Globe and an Oscar nomination for her leading role in the feature film *Ordinary People*. In 1986, I interviewed Moore about her latest film, *Just Between Friends*, produced by Moore's MTM Enterprises. Moore's career took off in 1961 after she was cast in the Emmy award-winning *Dick Van Dyke Show*. *The Mary Tyler Moore Show* debuted in 1970 and ran until 1977, with a record-breaking twenty-nine Emmy wins, four for Moore's role as Mary Richards.

LEFT

Romancing the Stone won a Golden Globe for Best Picture in 1985, putting Michael Douglas on the map as a Hollywood leading man and a savvy film producer. The film was so successful Douglas immediately produced and starred in a sequel, *The Jewel of the Nile.* In my 1984 interview with Douglas, we talked about his side career as a movie producer with a growing list of impressive credits for films such as *One Flew Over the Cuckoo's Nest,* which won an Academy Award for Best Picture in 1976, and *The China Syndrome,* which he also starred in.

LEFT

After her blazing film debut as the femme fatale in 1981's *Body Heat,* Kathleen Turner was cast in *Romancing the Stone.* I talked to Turner about working with Michael Douglas. The film resulted in Turner's first Golden Globe and a role in the follow-up film *The Jewel of the Nile* in 1985. Turner went on to star in *Prizzi's Honor,* which earned her a second Golden Globe, and in *Peggy Sue Got Married* (1986), which produced Oscar and Golden Globe nominations for her.

ABOVE LEFT

I interviewed Bette Midler backstage after her live concert in 1983 at the Fair Park Music Hall. Midler took a break from films after winning a Golden Globe and an Oscar nomination for her first feature film *The Rose* in 1979. She broke into show business as a singer, winning her first Grammy award in 1973 for her debut album *The Divine Miss M*. In 1977, she won an Emmy for her television special *Ol' Red Hair is Back*. She was nominated for a Golden Globe for her 1980 concert film *The Divine Miss M*.

ABOVE

Garry Marshall was one of Hollywood's sitcom wunderkinds, creating and producing the seminal series *Happy Days* and its seven spinoffs, including *Laverne and Shirley* and *Mork and Mindy*. In 1982, he began directing feature films, starting with *Young Doctors in Love*. I interviewed him in 1984 in LA about his second venture into directing, *The Flamingo Kid*. Marshall had also written the story and screenplay for the film, which became a blockbuster hit. More hit films were ahead, including *Beaches* and *Pretty Woman*.

ABOVE

I interviewed Scott Baio in 1984 about his new sitcom, *Charles in Charge*. When Baio was seventeen, he joined the cast of the sitcom *Happy Days*. Before the series ended in 1984, Baio's popular character Chachi was spun off to its own series, *Joanie Loves Chachi*. In 1976, Baio starred in the all-child-actors motion picture *Bugsy Malone* with Jodie Foster and appeared again with her in 1980's *Foxes*.

ABOVE LEFT

I interviewed Diane Lane in 1984 about her leading role in *The Cotton Club*, directed by Frances Ford Coppola. Lane grew up acting on stage in New York City. When she was thirteen, she was cast in her first film *A Little Romance*. In August 1979, when she was fourteen, she was featured on the cover of *Time* magazine with the banner headline "Hollywood's Whiz Kids." In 1983, Lane starred in *The Outsiders* and *Rumblefish,* also directed by Coppola. Both films featured a cast of emerging young adult actors, some of whom became known as the Brat Pack.

ABOVE

Gregory Hines was one of the male leads in 1984's *The Cotton Club*, a film based on the Mario Puzo novel. Hines talked to me about the film that was five years in the making and went famously over budget. Trained as a dancer, Hines received Tony nominations for his work in the Broadway musicals *Eubie!*, *Comin' Uptown*, and *Sophisticated Ladies*. In the 1980s, he won Emmys for the television specials *I Love Liberty* and *Motown Returns to the Apollo*. Mel Brooks directed Hines in a starring role in *History of the World, Part I*; it was Hines's first feature film.

ABOVE

I interviewed Emilio Estevez in 1985 about *St. Elmo's Fire*, considered one of the key films in the Brat Pack canon. Estevez is often recognized as the Pack's leader, going back to his teenage years when he made home movies with his brother, Charlie Sheen; the Penn Brothers, Sean and Chris; and the Lowe brothers, Rob and Chad. The Brat Pack was a loosely defined group that expanded in size and eventually included females. The Pack's first foray into the legitimate film world was 1983's *The Outsiders*, followed by *The Breakfast Club* in 1985.

ABOVE LEFT

One of Michael Keaton's earliest acting ventures was on *Mister Rogers' Neighborhood* in 1975. After moving to Los Angeles, Keaton parlayed a role in the short-lived television series *Working Stiffs* into starring roles in comedic feature films, starting with *Night Shift* in 1982 and *Mr. Mom* in 1983. In 1984, he talked to me about being cast in the lead role of *Johnny Dangerously*, a film parody of 1930s gangster movies.

ABOVE

The combination of Sylvester Stallone and Dolly Parton is a match only Hollywood could come up with. In LA, I interviewed the pair, who were cast in the 1984 comedy *Rhinestone*. The film was mercilessly panned by critics and failed to break even at the box office, but Parton managed to get two hit country songs off the soundtrack. Parton, one of country music's most successful recording artists, received Golden Globe nominations for her starring roles in the films *9 to 5* and *The Best Little Whorehouse in Texas*. When *Rhinestone* was released, Stallone had already starred in three *Rocky* films, and was preparing to star for the second time as John Rambo in *Rambo: First Blood Part II*.

ABOVE

Marilu Henner was cast in the female lead of the satirical *Johnny Dangerously*. During Henner's interview with me about the film, she talked about working with director Amy Heckerling, who had directed only one other feature film, *Fast Times at Ridgemont High*. Henner began her acting career on the stage in 1971, making her first film appearance in 1977 in *Between the Lines*. The next year she was cast in the highly regarded hit sitcom *Taxi*, which won eighteen Emmy awards and brought Henner five Golden Globe nominations.

ABOVE
Maximum security measures were taken during the 1984 press interviews
for *Give My Regards to Broad Street*, a feature film written by and starring
Paul McCartney. It was my first time to interview McCartney after the
1963 Beatles press conference in Dallas.

RIGHT
Phil Wygant went from staff announcer to lighting director to production manager and finally promotion director during his twenty-seven years with Channel 5.

was visible from the moment we arrived at the front entrance of the Beverly Hills Hotel to the moment we left. We had to have our credentials on us at all times. When we took the elevator to the floor where the interviews were held, there was security as we left the elevator and security in every room we were in. Paul was gracious and very cooperative. I did something I never did before or since with a star. I asked Paul to autograph a photograph for Libby Altwegg, our Channel 5 lighting director and the number one Beatles fan in the country. He couldn't have been nicer.

Technology was the big change in 1985. Film was out, and Betacam tape was in. Fax machines replaced the noisy, clacking teletype machines, and typewriters were replaced with desktop computers.

After my husband Phil was dismissed by the new station owners, he became very interested in computers. He spent one summer investigating and studying computers and then decided on a Texas Instruments computer called the TI PRO. By the time we had computers in the newsroom, Phil was a bona fide computer geek. I had nothing to do with this gigantic box, the size of a small refrigerator, which sat on top of his desk in our home office. In 1983 he had the first home computer of anyone we knew. He named it "Igor, because it's such a monster." I remember he cautioned me not to make any appointments for him on a certain Saturday because he was going to what he called "Igor Tech." It was a seminar to be held at the Texas Instruments offices in Dallas. Except for Igor Tech, he was self-taught. He and Igor would duke it out until one of them won. He discovered a flaw in one piece of software that had been on the market for some time, undetected. The manufacturer was impressed with this customer in Texas.

Christmas 1985 was enjoyed at our condo in St. Petersburg, Florida, on Tampa Bay. It was our traditional Christmas. Phil spent the first months of the New Year getting tax information together. In February 1986, he started feeling ill and showed signs of jaundice. The diagnosis was inconclusive. Tests showed no signs of cancer, but he kept getting weaker and weaker. On Monday, April 21, he was moved from a hospital in Fort Worth to Baylor Hospital in Dallas. Extensive tests were made Tuesday and a biopsy was scheduled for Wednesday, but in the night he took a turn for the worse and was placed in intensive care. He died Friday morning, April 25, 1986. A limited autopsy showed cancer to be the cause. It all happened so fast. I was devastated. My brother Carl and his wife Nancy flew in from Indiana Wednesday and were with me at the hospital. Losing Phil, my husband of thirty-eight years, was the absolute worst thing I could ever imagine. He was the love of my life. He was my everything. Our closest friends and I always called him

"Leader" because of the role he assumed on our various trips and adventures. He was the leader, we were his troop. Without Phil I was lost. I had no life.

I knew I had to get back to work, where I would have to concentrate on other things, or I would remain in a state of grief. Work was my therapy. Work and the two *fs* saved me—friends and faith. People were so helpful. One noon hour KXAS news anchor Jane McGarry went to my house and planted flowers in two large, empty pots at the front entrance. I hadn't had time to take care of them, and it was bothering me. I didn't know until later it was Jane who did that. I was surrounded by loving friends who helped in so many ways.

Faith was the other *f*. Born a "cradle Catholic," my faith has always been important in my life. Prayer is as natural to me as eating meals. I can't imagine my life without it. Prayer was the reason I was able to get on with my life without Phil. My motto is, "We're still together. For now, we're just in different places."

In 1991, Harold Taft, our chief meteorologist, died after battling cancer for several years. It was a huge loss to Channel 5 and to his thousands of loyal viewers. When Harold started *Weather Telefacts* with Walter Porter and Bob Denney in 1949, we shared an office for a brief time. Harold and I also cohosted the Jerry Lewis Telethon for sixteen years. Harold ran the weather department like the military. He served as an officer in the Air Force and as a colonel in the Texas Air National Guard. My favorite memories are of the times late at night, after the midnight news, when I was working late. After LIN

ABOVE LEFT
Starting in 1977, I was one of the hosts on the Jerry Lewis MDA Labor Day Telethon for the Muscular Dystrophy Association. The annual weekend-long show aired on Channel 5 for thirty-eight years.

ABOVE
Harold Taft (center) and I were the local emcees for the annual telethon for sixteen years. Other Channel 5 personalities pitched in, too, including Bill Kelley (on left in black tuxedo) and sportscaster Scott Murray (on right in black tuxedo).

RIGHT
Chief meteorologist Harold Taft was known for his hand-drawn weather maps and no-nonsense delivery of the weather forecast. "The World's Greatest Weatherman" managed to survive management's attempt to mothball him, but he did not win his battle with cancer.

bought the station, Harold would come and stand in my doorway so he could listen for the phone in his office down the hall. He would give me reports on what the second floor suits wanted to do. It was always something Harold considered ridiculous, and he would laugh and laugh. Nobody messed with the weather department. The Colonel wasn't having it. When a news director wanted to discuss some "new ideas," Harold ignored the request. At one time a report circulated that the new owners wanted to replace Harold Taft. The station was bombarded with complaints. Advertisers threatened to take their business elsewhere. Bumper stickers appeared declaring "I believe Harold."

In 1988 Doug Adams left the news department to move into management. Within a short time LIN made him president and general manager of its station in Decatur, Illinois. The following year they moved him to WAVY in Portsmouth-Norfolk, to be president and general manager. In 1991 LIN brought Doug Adams back to Fort Worth-Dallas to be president and general manager of KXAS-TV. It was the happiest news we'd had in a long time. At a welcome-back reception I remember whispering to Doug, "There is a TV God."

The following year, in 1992, with Jane McGarry and Mike Snyder as anchors of the six and ten o'clock news programs, ratings went from third place to number one and remained there for many years. Mike had joined the station as a reporter in 1979, and Jane McGarry as a reporter in 1982, and by 1990 they were coanchors. They lasted through 2010—the longest-running news anchor duo in Texas TV broadcast history.

Television film critics were increasing in numbers throughout the country. Press tours in the 1990s could have thirty to forty people invited for interviews. The only way to accommodate that many journalists was to cut the time for each interview. In the '60s and '70s we might get as much as ten minutes for interviews. You could give viewers more than a plug for the new film. You could discuss issues, and past movies, and how they related to today's roles. You could have fun with the stars. With five minutes or less, the interviewer had to ask questions that didn't require long answers. You didn't want the star to take up the entire time answering one question.

In 1995 a group of TV critics including Jim Ferguson from Tucson, Arizona; Sara Voorhees from Albuquerque, New Mexico; and John De Simio and Joey Berlin from Los Angeles formed the Broadcast Film Critics' Association to give Critics' Choice Awards for achievements in film. The early membership included Bill Carlson and Nancy Nelson from Minneapolis; Harry Martin from Sacramento; Gino Salomone from Milwaukee; Pat Stoner from Philadelphia; and me. From the first awards luncheon in a small hotel dining room the organization has grown to over three hundred TV, radio, and online film critics. We keep outgrowing venues. Currently the Critics' Choice Awards are held in an events venue that used to be an airport hangar in Santa Monica. Stars and studio bigwigs attend in such numbers there is hardly room for members.

In 2000 I was surprised to receive the Critics' Choice Critic Award in Los Angeles, in which the critics honor one of their own members. I had no clue I was the recipient until my competition at WFAA-TV in Dallas, my friend Gary Cogill, started the introduction. I started to panic, wondering *what am I going to say when I get to the podium?* Why didn't somebody tell me? I made it to the stage and received the award from Gary. As I faced the audience, seated directly below me was Steven Spielberg. I started my acceptance by saying that one of the rewards of being in this

ABOVE LEFT
In 1990, Mike Snyder and Jane McGarry were introduced as the lead KXAS-TV anchors. Promoted as JAM (Jane and Mike), they became the longest-running news anchor duo in Texas TV history.

ABOVE LEFT

Michael Caine talked to me in 1986 about working with director Woody Allen on *Hannah and Her Sisters*. The film was nominated for seven Oscars, including Best Picture; Caine ended up winning for best supporting actor. He started acting on the London stage in the 1950s and began appearing on TV and in British films in the 1960s, including *The Ipcress File* and *Alfie,* for which he was nominated for an Oscar. Caine received a second Academy Award nomination for his lead role in 1972's *Sleuth.* In 1983, he won a Golden Globe award for best actor in *Educating Rita.*

ABOVE

Hannah and her Sisters gave actress Barbara Hershey the opportunity to work in a film that is considered to be one of director Woody Allen's best. After appearing in a string of made-for-TV movies in the 1970s, Hershey told me that moving from LA to New York helped to ignite her career; she landed starring roles in *The Stunt Man, The Entity, The Right Stuff*, and *The Natural.*

ABOVE

Carrie Fisher made her screen debut in *Shampoo* when she was eighteen. Two years later, she was cast as Princess Leia in *Star Wars* and reprised the role in 1980's *The Empire Strikes Back* and 1983's *Return of the Jedi.* I caught up with Fisher again in 1986 to talk about working in the ensemble cast of Woody Allen's *Hannah and Her Sisters*, one of Allen's highest-grossing films.

LEFT

I talked with Willem Dafoe in 1986 about his supporting role in *Platoon*, for which he received an Oscar nomination. Before filming began, Dafoe and the rest of the cast endured thirty days of rigorous boot camp military training in the Philippines. *Platoon* was honored with four Academy Awards including best picture. Dafoe began his acting career off-Broadway as one of the founding members of the Wooster Group.

LEFT

After an extended delay, Oliver Stone's film *Platoon* finally went into production in 1986. Emilio Estevez had been cast in one of the lead roles, but due to scheduling conflicts he was no longer available to play the part. His younger brother Charlie Sheen ended up being cast. It was his first major film role. I interviewed Sheen about the hurdles of filming on location in the jungles of the Philippines.

ABOVE

I interviewed Danny DeVito about directing and starring in *Throw Momma from the Train*, his second time to direct. DeVito appeared twice in *One Flew Over the Cuckoo's Nest*, first on the off-Broadway stage and also in its screen adaptation, which swept the 1976 Academy Awards. DeVito won an Emmy and a Golden Globe for his breakout role in the TV sitcom *Taxi,* which ran from 1978 until 1983. He transitioned to film roles that included *Terms of Endearment, Romancing the Stone,* and *The Jewel of the Nile.* His role in *Ruthless People* gained him a Golden Globe nomination.

ABOVE LEFT

When comedian Billy Crystal was cast as a lead in *Throw Momma From the Train*, he was not yet a household name, but he was getting close. I interviewed Crystal about the black comedy in 1987 at a press preview in Palm Springs. Crystal's first career break came in 1977 when he was cast in the TV sitcom *Soap.* The next year he made his film debut in a starring role in Joan Rivers's *Rabbit Test.* His network variety show *The Billy Crystal Comedy Hour* was cancelled after two airings, but he joined the cast of *Saturday Night Live* for a season in 1985. He starred in *Running Scared* and played a memorable costarring role in *The Princess Bride.*

ABOVE

Kevin Costner's career was gaining momentum when he was cast in the starring role of 1987's political thriller *No Way Out.* We talked at the film's press preview in Washington, DC, about the film's inside-Washington plot line and working with costars Gene Hackman and Sean Young. Earlier in the year, Costner starred as Eliot Ness in the box office hit *The Untouchables.* The thirty-two-year-old actor had a big career ahead of him.

ABOVE

Actor David Hasselhoff had success starring in several television series, including *The Young and the Restless* and *Knight Rider*. In 1989, I interviewed him as his next television series *Baywatch* was about to debut. After *Baywatch*'s first season, NBC canceled the show. Hasselhoff put up his own money and with investors brought the show back to life, selling it through the first-run television syndication market. *Baywatch* found its audience and became a massive hit, with Hasselhoff as executive producer.

ABOVE LEFT

Like Annette Bening, Colin Firth was at the beginning of his film career when director Miloš Forman cast him as the male lead in *Valmont*. What he lacked in screen credits he more than made up for with years in leading roles on the London stage and in British television dramas. Firth and a group of talented young British actors on the rise in the late 1980s, including Gary Oldman, Daniel Day Lewis, Tim Roth, Bruce Payne, Spencer Lee, and Paul McGann, were labeled "The Brit Pack."

ABOVE

When I interviewed Annette Bening for 1989's *Valmont,* I discovered it was only her second film. Despite Bening's lack of film experience, director Miloš Forman was impressed with her classical stage training, which included working with the Colorado Shakespeare Festival Company, the San Diego Repertory Theatre, and the American Conservatory Theater in San Francisco. In 1987, Bening was nominated for a Tony for her Broadway debut in *Coastal Disturbances*. Her first film appearance was in the 1988 comedy *The Great Outdoors*, starring Dan Aykroyd and John Candy.

ABOVE

By the time Meg Tilly was cast in *Valmont*, she had starred in *The Big Chill, Agnes of God,* and four other feature films. During my interview with Tilly we talked about her early ballet career, which came to a halt when her back was injured after her partner dropped her. *Valmont* was based on the same French novel as Stephen Frears's *Dangerous Liasons,* which came out a year before. Frears's film did great box office and won three Oscars. *Valmont*, considered by some to be the superior film, came up short on awards and at the box office.

ABOVE

Colors was the fourth film that actor Dennis Hopper directed. He talked to me in LA in 1988 about casting the young Sean Penn with screen veteran Robert Duval. Hopper had recently revived his unconventional acting career by playing a memorable villain in David Lynch's *Blue Velvet* and an Oscar-nominated supporting role in *Hoosiers*. He started acting in the 1950s in notable films such as *Rebel Without a Cause*, *Giant*, and *Gunflight at the OK Corral*. He made almost 150 appearances in episodic television before famously directing and starring in the epic motorcycle road movie *Easy Rider* in 1969.

ABOVE LEFT

In 1986, Vincent Price was cast in the lead of Walt Disney Pictures' animated film *The Great Mouse Detective*. Even though the part was in voice only, Price told me Professor Ratigan was one of his favorite characters to play. That's saying something for an actor who started his career in 1935 performing on the stage with Orson Welles's Mercury Theatre and played more than one hundred different characters over his career. Price is most often associated with the horror genre, starring in *The House of Wax*, *The Fly*, *The Tingler,* and *The House of Usher*, among many others. He also appeared in comedies and dramas, notably 1944's film noir classic *Laura*.

ABOVE

When I interviewed Martin Landau in 1988 he expressed gratitude to director Frances Ford Coppola for reviving his career by casting him in a supporting role in *Tucker: The Man and His Dream*. Landau won a Golden Globe and an Academy Award nomination for his work in the film. One of Landau's first appearances on the big screen was as a villain in Alfred Hitchcock's classic *North by Northwest*. He was in the cast of television's *Mission Impossible* and was a familiar face on dramatic and episodic television shows throughout the 1950s and 60s.

ABOVE
Gary Cogill, film critic for WFAA-TV in Dallas, and I during a 1999 press trip to Edinburgh, Scotland.

ABOVE RIGHT
Director Steven Spielberg attended the Critics' Choice Awards show in Los Angeles in 2000, when he received the Director of the Decade award and I was honored with the Critics' Critic award.

business over a period of time is watching young talent develop into major players. Then I recounted being invited to a luncheon in Los Angeles some years ago. The studio was announcing new films in development, but there would be no interviews. The luncheon on a hotel rooftop was very pleasant. At one point a studio executive came over and said, "In a moment I'm going to bring a young man over here and seat him next to you. Just talk about anything." So this fuzzy-faced little guy sat down and I asked him if he worked at Universal Studios. He said he was starting to direct some things for TV but he hoped to direct movies. He said he had been making movies since he was twelve years old. I made a mental note of that young man's name because I knew that one day he would be famous. I continued my impromptu speech by saying, "And he is famous. That fuzzy-faced guy is seated in front of me. He is Steven Spielberg!" Later in the program a Critics' Choice Award went to Steven Spielberg as Director of the Decade. A reporter covering the event noted that Spielberg and I received the only standing ovations that night.

The Dallas Morning News

High Profile

Sunday, October 25, 1998   ©1998, The Dallas Morning News   The Archive http://archive.dallasnews.com   Section E

Channel 5 and entertainment reporter Bobbie Wygant went on the air together in 1948.

The Dallas Morning News: Natalie Caudill

BOBBIE WYGANT

After 50 years on Channel 5, she's primed to keep on ticking

 Roberta would never do.

Too downbeat. Uncarbonated. The Franciscan nuns used it on her in grade school. But at home and to the world at large, she was and has always been Bobbie. Effervescent. Indomitable. And present at the creation of the Southwest's first television station, then WBAP, now KXAS. Better known as Channel 5.

"A remarkable journey," Bobbie Wygant says. "I have been blessed to be along for the entire ride."

It's been rocky at times. New Year's Eve 1974, for instance. Husband Philip, who brought her to Channel 5 with him in 1948, came home that night with news that he'd been fired by the new station manager. They agreed that Bobbie should soldier on without him.

Later in the decade, a news director intent on cleaning house thought the station should dispense with Ms. Wygant and her entertainment beat. Think again.

"I've got a lot of blood, sweat, tears and toil invested here," she remembers telling him. "And I ain't leavin'."

She hasn't. And as Channel 5 and Ms. Wygant mark their 50th anniversary together, she's hoping to turn at least one last corner in an incredible on-camera career.

"If I make it to the millennium, my epitaph could be 'She Spent Two Centuries in Television.' That would look good on a headstone, wouldn't it?"

Continued on page 4

Bobbie Wygant (left) interviews actress Jane Fonda for Channel 5's *Dateline* program.

Photo Courtesy of Channel 5

"I'm not going to trash a movie just to get in a bunch of cute one-liners. I think there's a way of letting an audience know why you don't like a film without getting nasty about it. People really wouldn't accept that very well from me if I'm suddenly up there being Joan Rivers."

— **Bobbie Wygant**

BY ED BARK

THIRTEEN

Golden Anniversary

The year 1998 marked my fiftieth anniversary with Channel 5. Marian Norman had the desk next to mine in the newsroom. When she learned about my golden anniversary, she said, "We have to have a big celebration."

OPPOSITE
The 1998 *Dallas Morning News* article about my fifty years in television was icing on the cake.

I was against it, but finally gave in when she said station manager Doug Adams agreed with her. What really made me give in was that Casa Mañana, Fort Worth's musical theater, wanted to name a scholarship to its theater school in my honor. I liked that idea, but I urged Marian to keep the celebration a simple, low-key affair. Beyond that I wanted no part in planning the anniversary.

On the day of the luncheon I arrived at the Radisson Hotel in downtown Fort Worth and was surprised to see tables with auction items on display. I figured it was for the scholarship fund. At noon the doors opened to what I thought would be a nice little luncheon.

I couldn't believe my eyes! It was a large ballroom with wall-to-wall tables, decorations galore, and a stage with a huge "Bobbie" backdrop and screens for tape projections. What was going on here? I was overwhelmed!

Marian and her committee had sold tables at a hefty price to advertising agencies, civic groups, and various arts organizations. Many movie studios sent vice presidents with tributes and gifts. It was a panorama of people I knew throughout my fifty years with the station. Monsignor Joseph Schumacher, a former pastor and Vicar General of the Catholic Diocese of Fort Worth, gave the invocation.

A TRIBUTE HONORING
Bobbie Wygant

ABOVE
The program cover for my golden
anniversary luncheon.

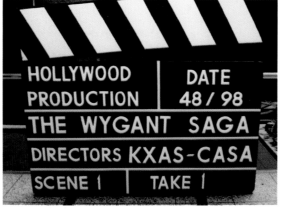

HOLLYWOOD PRODUCTION | DATE 48 / 98
THE WYGANT SAGA
DIRECTORS KXAS-CASA
SCENE 1 | TAKE 1

ABOVE
The tribute luncheon was nothing short of a Hollywood
production with singers and dancers and video tributes
from friends and stars.

BELOW
Me at the tribute luncheon with Ruta Lee (left) and longtime
friends from the TV station (second from left to right): Libby
Altwegg, Carmen Vasquez, and Christina Patoski.

RIGHT
The Radisson Hotel ballroom was wall-to-wall tables with a big screen TV to show the special documentary that Channel 5 made about me.

FAR RIGHT
An elaborate stage show was written, directed, and performed by Joel Ferrell and the Casa Mañana crew.

RIGHT
Ruta Lee flew in from Los Angeles to star in the salute.

FAR RIGHT
KXAS-TV reporter Marian Norman (left) cochaired the luncheon and KXAS news anchor Brad Wright (center) emceed.

RIGHT
The lavish event left me nearly speechless.

LEFT
I always have fun with *Greater Tuna*'s Joe Sears (left) and Jaston Williams. They videotaped a special *Tuna* tribute to me that was shown at the luncheon.

Various coworkers spoke, among them anchors Brad Wright and Chip Moody. It was all too much. Joel Ferrell, a director of Casa Mañana productions, had singers and dancers from Casa doing specially written material in a mini musical. And the big surprise—Ruta Lee came from Los Angeles. Ruta played more leading roles at Casa Mañana for more years than any other actress. Thankfully, Ruta poked fun at me to balance the sweet talk of other speakers. During her many years of starring in Casa shows, Ruta and I became close friends. I attend her yearly fundraising events for the Thalians charity in Los Angeles.

The Tuna Texas guys, Joe Sears and Jaston Williams, taped vignettes written especially for my fiftieth anniversary. These hilarious skits were projected on screens throughout the program. Sears and Williams are two of the most talented, most versatile actors and writers in all of show business.

Steve Moffett, who directed many of my shows, including my Academy Awards specials, put together a documentary of my fifty years at Channel 5. It was beautifully crafted and very entertaining. The audience loved it.

Letters and greetings were read from many stars, including Tom Cruise, John Travolta, and Tom Hanks. The big surprise was an on-camera message from Bob Hope taped in the rose garden at his Toluca Lake home. At the end he said, "When you reach another fifty, Bobbie, then we'll talk." Bob was ninety-five at the time and still making appearances. In his eyes I was a pup. He ended his message with "Dolores sends love."

A special thrill for me was that my French friends Ann and Serge Lorsery surprised me and came from Paris for the celebration. Their cousin and my longtime Fort Worth friend Colette Miller tipped them off.

RIGHT
Awards started rolling in, including the Women in Communications' Trailblazer Award.

FAR RIGHT
I was inducted into the Gold Circle of the National Academy of Television Arts & Sciences in 2004, joining the ranks of Walter Cronkite and other broadcast legends.

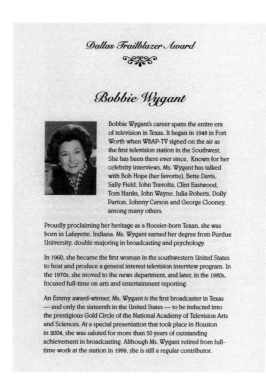

Dallas Trailblazer Award

Bobbie Wygant

Bobbie Wygant's career spans the entire era of television in Texas. It began in 1948 in Fort Worth when WBAP-TV signed on the air as the first television station in the Southwest. She has been there ever since. Known for her celebrity interviews, Ms. Wygant has talked with Bob Hope (her favorite), Bette Davis, Sally Field, John Travolta, Clint Eastwood, Tom Hanks, John Wayne, Julia Roberts, Dolly Parton, Johnny Carson and George Clooney, among many others.

Proudly proclaiming her heritage as a Hoosier-born Texan, she was born in Lafayette, Indiana. Ms. Wygant earned her degree from Purdue University, double majoring in broadcasting and psychology.

In 1960, she became the first woman in the southwestern United States to host and produce a general interest television interview program. In the 1970s, she moved to the news department, and later, in the 1980s, focused full-time on arts and entertainment reporting.

An Emmy award-winner, Ms. Wygant is the first broadcaster in Texas — and only the sixteenth in the United States — to be inducted into the prestigious Gold Circle of the National Academy of Television Arts and Sciences. At a special presentation that took place in Houston in 2004, she was saluted for more than 50 years of outstanding achievement in broadcasting. Although Ms. Wygant retired from full-time work at the station in 1999, she is still a regular contributor.

When I got to the podium to speak, I explained that all of this was a total surprise. I thought it was going to be a nice little luncheon. I thanked Marian Norman, chairman of the event, as well as Ramona Logan and everyone at the station who helped her. I felt guilty that I was so disinterested and not in the least cooperative. To show you how disinterested I was, I accepted an invitation to go to New York that weekend to do interviews with Anthony Hopkins and Marcia Gay Hardin for the movie *Meet Joe Black*. My bags were packed and in the trunk of my car. I drove directly from the celebration to DFW Airport.

I'm still apologizing for my attitude, but let it be known that from that day until this day I deeply appreciate all their efforts in giving me one of the most rewarding experiences of my life. And I'm proud that the Bobbie Wygant Scholarship is still helping young students study theater arts at Casa Mañana's school.

There were other surprises to come. In 1999 the Dallas chapter of Women in Film gave me a Lifetime Achievement Award. Much of my work focused on interviewing actors and filmmakers and reviewing films.

In 2004 a huge surprise came out of the blue. I was invited to Houston to be inducted into the Gold Circle of the National Academy of Television Arts and Sciences. It was a special Emmy for fifty years of outstanding contributions to the television broadcast community. It would add me to an elite group that included Walter Cronkite. I have never applied for any award. I couldn't imagine how this came about. Eventually I learned that our vice president of news, Susan Tully, asked Reginald Hardwick, one of our news producers, to make the application. Reginald was the producer of many newscasts in which my entertainment reports ran. My dear friend Betty Bob Buckley accompanied me to Houston. George Pennacchio, Entertainment Reporter for KABC Los Angeles, flew to Houston for the occasion.

LEFT
The Alliance for Women
in Media's Gracie Awards
ceremony was in
New York City in 2014.

The Dallas Chapter of Women in Communications presented me with its Dallas Trailblazer Award in 2008. I was a longtime member of WIC. Each year in Fort Worth I emceed its all-female Celebrity Breakfast featuring such guest celebrities as Barbara Walters, Erma Bombeck, and Lady Bird Johnson.

The Dallas Press Club included me in its first group of Living Legends in 2011. In 2014 I went to New York to accept a Gracie Award from the Alliance for Women in Media. I appreciate all awards, from paper certificates to big plaques. While I will never apply, it would make me very happy if one day I could be inducted into the Broadcasting Hall of Fame.

But enough already about awards. Back at the TV station there were rumors that NBC was going to buy our station from LIN Broadcasting. Really? The sale happened in 1998. NBC had always been our network, but KXAS-TV was an affiliate station, not owned and operated by the NBC network. Now we would be an O&O.

It was joyful news. I didn't know anybody who was sad about seeing LIN go. There was, however, one good thing about LIN. Those who participated in LIN's stock option plan and sold their LIN stock before NBC took over made big profits. I'm told some engineers who were paid union wages and sold their LIN stock before the NBC sale came out millionaires. I sold my stock for a nice big check, but nothing near a million. This would not have happened in the early days when WBAP-TV was a privately held, family-owned company.

From the day the NBC network arrived, my job changed. I immediately had to stop press trips because NBC did not allow reporters to accept free travel and accommodations in exchange for interviews. The station had to pay all expenses. The problem was that the station

RIGHT
I was in the Dallas Press Club's first group of Living Legends honorees in 2011.

didn't have the money or didn't want to spend the money for these celebrity interviews.

In 1999 Doug Adams left as president and manager of KXAS-TV and joined the Dallas Symphony Orchestra as general manager.

I knew it was time for me to leave Channel 5. If I couldn't travel, I couldn't get what I needed for my entertainment reports. While stars sometimes came to Dallas-Fort Worth, their trips didn't happen often enough to feed my daily stories.

On my last day in 1999, News Director Kim Godwin came to me and said, "Before you leave, Steve Doerr wants to see you." Doerr was the new station manager hired by NBC. He greeted me pleasantly and came from behind his desk and sat in a chair across from me.

"We want you to stay, Bobbie. We can tear up this retirement paperwork if you'll stay."

I said, "Steve, I appreciate your offer, but I have to leave. I can no longer do what it is I do, celebrity interviews. The only way I can get the celebrities is to do the press trips offered by the film studios. But," I continued, "I want to keep an open door. I have no hard feelings. I don't agree with your rules, but I respect your right to make them."

He agreed that the station would keep an open door as well. We shook hands and parted friends. Some staff members thought the station was concerned that my leaving could create a public relations problem and possibly a

LEFT
Comedienne Phyllis Diller
and I developed a warm rapport
after knowing each other for
more than forty years.

charge of age discrimination. My leaving made the front page of the *Fort Worth Star-Telegram* and the Dallas papers as well, but my statement to all inquiries was that leaving was my decision; that the station wanted me to stay but that I left because under NBC rules, I could no longer do my job.

There was one amusing thing about my leaving the station. Corporate NBC had our human resources manager, Martha Stallard, show me a catalog and ask me to choose a retirement gift. I chose a gold wristwatch. It's a very good watch by Tissot. My jeweler says in the trade it's called a "baby Rolex." When it came many weeks later, the back was engraved "Robert Wygant 50 years." Martha insisted we send it back, but I wouldn't let her. I thought it embodied the philosophy of a big corporation where an employ-

ee is a number. A name doesn't really matter. Roberta is my legal name, but I'm known professionally and to 99 percent of the population as Bobbie. To NBC, however, I'll always be Robert.

I never really considered myself retired. To me I was on a sabbatical. I would see a star on TV, and I'd remember interviews I had done with him or her. I remember seeing Phyllis Diller on a late-night show, and I recalled what happened the first time I interviewed her. We had time to talk before the show, and she told me she was going to have a facelift that would include a nose job. She went into great detail. When we did the interview we talked about a show she was doing in Dallas and about Bob Hope. She and the Hopes were very close friends. She said that no matter the time of day or night, if she heard a joke she thought Bob

RIGHT
Conductor Richard Kaufman and
I became good friends when he
was the Dallas Symphony's pops
conductor, a friendship that
continues to this day.

hadn't heard, she would call him and tell him
the joke. Bob was a night person, so she paid no
attention to the time. It was a fun interview.

A day or so later I saw her on a network show
and the reporter asked her what she thought
about plastic surgery. This was at a time when
stars went to great lengths to hide that they
ever had a nip or tuck. Phyllis launched into the
same story she had given me a few days earlier.
She said "This is the first time I've talked about
having a facelift on the air." I was furious with
myself. I could have had a scoop, and I blew it!

Now that I didn't have to keep a schedule, I
spent time traveling abroad and staying at our
Florida condo. I went to movies I wanted to see
rather than movies I had to see. I spent more
time with longtime close friends, especially Kiki
Smith, Drake Benthall, Shirley and Louis Daniel, and Harry and Colette Miller. Our friendships went back to the fifties.

A few months after leaving the station, I answered a phone call. It was Kim Godwin from
KXAS-TV. She said they were going to start a
new program called *First at Four*. It would be

the first 4 p.m. news program in the market. Jeff
Eliasoph and Deborah Ferguson would be the
anchors. They would like to have some entertainment reports. Would I do them?

I was caught off guard but I managed to say,
"Not every day."

Kim came back, "How many would you do?"

I was flummoxed but I said, "Maybe one or
two a week, but I have to think about it and see
what's available."

She said, "I'll call you back tomorrow."

I was walking out the door when I took her
call, so I drove to Dallas for the opening of *The
Sound of Music,* starring Florence Henderson.
When I entered the Music Hall at Fair Park the
first person I saw was Michael Jenkins, president and general manager of the Dallas Summer Musicals. I told him about Kim's phone
call, and he said, "Oh please go back. Channel 5
hasn't mentioned us since you left."

I knew Florence Henderson from previous
interviews, so Michael Jenkins arranged a time,
and I was able to have Florence for the premiere
of *First at Four*. I was no longer on sabbatical.
From that day until this I have been doing reports for NBC 5/KXAS-TV on a freelance basis.
I hope to match or break Walter Cronkite's sev-
enty-three years in broadcasting.

I've always loved symphonies, but when I
was working my 24/7 schedule I rarely had time
for symphony concerts. I saw an ad for a pops
concert at the Meyerson Symphony Center in
Dallas with Richard Kaufman, conductor. The
name rang a bell. Whenever I saw NBC *Today Show* entertainment reporter Jim Brown
on press tours, he would ask me if I ever interviewed Richard Kaufman, pops conductor of the
Dallas Symphony. He and Kaufman were good
friends. Brown said, "Kaufman was a musician
with MGM for years, and he has great stories."

When I set up the interview through the
Symphony's PR people, I said, "Be sure to tell
Mr. Kaufman that Jim Brown has been after me
for years to interview him."

When I met Richard Kaufman it was instant friendship. Kaufman guest-conducts major symphonies throughout the United States and all over the world. He served as principal pops conductor of the Dallas Symphony for fourteen years. His fulltime job for twenty-six years has been principal pops conductor of Orange County Pacific Symphony. I joined Richard and his wife Gayle when he conducted the Chicago Symphony in a tribute to Roger Ebert.

Before I ever began reviewing films, the critic I looked up to was Roger Ebert. The music that night was selected by Roger. After the concert I was able to talk with him. We had met on press tours, but this evening occurred after Roger had cancer operations and was no longer able to speak. He communicated with writing and hand signals. I cherish the memories of that special night in Chicago.

In 2001 the Dallas Summer Musicals starred Ann-Margret in *The Best Little Whorehouse in Texas*. I had interviewed Ann-Margret several times. She was a delight and very good in interviews. Except for the first time.

In 1961 I got a call from Hal Bakke, who represented RCA Victor Records in Dallas. Hal used to be an announcer at WBAP Radio. He told me that RCA was sending a new young singer to Dallas-Fort Worth to promote her first recording, called "Lost Love." He said he had never heard of her, but he understood that she had performed with George Burns on stage in Las Vegas. I figured if George Burns liked her she couldn't be bad, so I agreed to interview this Ann-Margret with no last name.

It was a taped interview. When I introduced her and asked the first question, she replied, but so quietly that I could barely hear her. Johnny Hay was directing us. After a bit he broke in on the loudspeaker and in a polite way asked her to please speak louder. We started again, and she was a little more

audible, but barely. Johnny stopped the tape and came out of the control room into the studio. He positioned her microphone a little closer to her mouth to see if that would help. We started a third time, but the problem was still there. So Johnny called maintenance and asked them to turn off the studio air conditioning fans. That helped enough that finally we could hear what she was saying. I felt sorry for her because she was trying hard to do a good interview. With her beauty and sweet manner, it was watchable TV. I understood the problem after her mother, Mrs. Olsson, told me that this was the very first TV interview Ann-Margret had ever done. During my half century of celebrity interviews I don't recall another one like Ann Margret's. Because film studios relied more and more on television to promote their films, actors and performers were required to do TV interviews. They had to learn how to talk without a script. Celebrities like Robin Williams, Jim Carrey, Joan Rivers, Phyllis Diller, and Don Rickles could do both at the same time—give a good interview and an entertaining performance. Tom Hanks, John Travolta, Helen Mirren, and Ron Howard might not go for laughs, but they'd make you sit up and take notice.

ABOVE
Roger Ebert was my favorite film critic.

OPPOSITE
I first interviewed Ann-Margret in 1961 when she was a soft-spoken young recording artist. As she blossomed into a full-fledged actress and singer, I interviewed her many times over the years.

FOURTEEN

Leaving Broadcast Hill

My husband's mother was an admirable, wise woman who was widowed in her early forties and was left to run a business and raise two boys. Since I lost my mother and later my grandmother, Phil's mother was a special gift to me.

OPPOSITE
The WBAP-TV studios on Broadcast Hill in 1952.

I loved her dearly. She often said, "The things we worry about are not the things that happen. It's always the things that come from left field, the things you couldn't ever imagine, these are the things that change your life."

I immediately thought of her when we first heard that Carter Publications was selling the station in 1974 to LIN Broadcasting, and again in 1998 when NBC Network bought the station.

Another shock hit in 2012 when NBC announced that we would leave our original Fort Worth location on Broadcast Hill to move into a brand-new facility near DFW Airport. Who saw that coming?

As moving day drew closer, I was asked to do a news feature where I would tour the studios, control rooms, and newsroom and reflect on my sixty-five years working in this original building.

Walking into the big studio and thinking about the many interviews I did there brought a flood of memories. For some reason, one of the first flashbacks was from 1968. Tricia and Julie Nixon came for an interview on behalf of their father's presidential campaign. In *LIFE* magazine that year there was a double-page spread showing Richard and Pat Nixon in a receiving line and the two Nixon daughters in front of them. All four were laughing uproariously. I asked the Nixon girls what

LEFT
Groundbreaking day in 2012
for the new KXAS-TV building,
just south of the Dallas-Fort
Worth Airport.

was so funny. They said that their parents had been in the line for a long time shaking one hand after another. The girls thought it would be funny if they got in line. When they approached their parents and extended their hands it took a second or two for the parents to realize, "Oh my gosh, these are our girls!" They all broke up and the photographer caught all four exploding with laughter.

Another memory was my first meeting with Charlton Heston. He was promoting *Will Penny*, a western movie that received very good reviews. I was taping a short radio feature before the live TV interview. I remember how disinterested Heston seemed to be in the radio interview, but I thought he would get up to speed for live TV. Wrong! To begin with, he sprawled out in the chair with his head back out of camera range. His answer to my first question was, "Well," (long pause) "I don't know." (another pause) "I suppose." This went on for fifteen to twenty seconds, which can be an eternity in TV time. Finally he straightened up and took a little more interest in the interview but not in a way I expected. After all, this was Charlton

Heston, Ben Hur, the current president of the Screen Actors Guild. What's wrong with you? I had done an extra amount of preparation. I knew my questions were good. You'd think as a producer and star of the film he would be enthusiastic to the max.

After he left I called the local press representative to find out what was wrong with Mr. Heston. After some coaxing and putting pressure, I learned that Mr. Heston had arrived around midnight the night before and said that he didn't want to do any press the next morning because he had a tennis date at the Dallas Country Club. The studio representative explained that he had approved his schedule and that the next morning was full with newspaper columnists on deadline and a live TV show. These could not be canceled. So Heston had to reschedule the tennis date, and he wasn't happy about it.

Some weeks later I received a call from another studio inviting me to New Orleans to interview Charlton Heston! "Bobbie, isn't this fantastic?" I quickly told the studio rep of my recent experience with Mr. Heston.

I said, "I'll get back to you." This apparently

RIGHT
Tricia (left) and Julie Nixon came
to the Channel 5 studios in
September 1968 for an interview
with me. The sisters were on the
campaign trail for their father, who
was running for president of the
United States. Two months later, on
November 5, 1968, Richard M. Nixon
was elected president, beating
incumbent vice president
Hubert Humphrey.

RIGHT
When I interviewed Charlton Heston
in 1973 for the dystopic thriller
Soylent Green, he had already
amassed an impressive list of
starring roles in major Hollywood
films of the 1950s and 60s, notably
The Ten Commandments, *Planet of
the Apes*, and *Ben-Hur,* which won
eleven Academy Awards, including
one for Heston.

set off alarm bells throughout the studios. I finally decided to go to New Orleans. I must admit I figured if the interview was a bust I'd still get a couple of fabulous New Orleans meals.

We arrived in New Orleans and were taken to the Court of Two Sisters for lunch with the stars of *Number One*, a movie in which Heston played an aging quarterback with the New Orleans Saints. I was ushered to a table and next thing I knew I was seated between Charlton Heston and his wife, Lydia, a professional photographer and delightful woman. Heston was all charm, meeting every press person one-on-one. At the end of each interview he said, "Did you get what you needed?" Talk about damage control! What a change from the interview he did in our studio. I interviewed Heston many times after that, and they all were what you want from Charlton Heston. We became friends, but neither of us ever mentioned our initial meeting. I wrote it off as "anyone can have a bad day."

I did numerous interviews with Robin Williams over the years. Robin's interviews were whatever you wanted. You want a serious discussion, he gave you serious answers. He must have had a photographic memory. He could recall dates and facts instantly. He was up on every current event. You never knew what to expect from him.

In one interview I was wearing a royal blue silk dress. He commented on it and I said at the station we called it my "chroma key blue dress" because at that time we were using a blue screen on which to project backgrounds. I could not wear the blue dress if we were using the blue screen because the dress would disappear.

My first question to Robin that day was, "Your mind doesn't work like anyone else's. I'd love to crawl inside your brain and see what you have the rest of us don't have."

With that, he took off doing a whole skit

LEFT
Robin Williams with Jeff Bridges (lower right) in *The Fisher King*, 1991. Williams's interviews were as wild as the crazy characters he played.
© 1991 TriStar Pictures, Inc. All rights reserved. Courtesy of TriStar Pictures.

about a little lady in a chroma key blue dress. "Oh she's getting inside my brain and she's looking around. Oops honey. Careful, you nearly tripped over my frontal lobe." He carried on for a full minute or so. It was a hilarious performance!

When we did interviews in New York in 1991 for *The Fisher King*, Robin got wound up telling me a story about a homeless person who somehow wandered onto the set and was insisting that Robin let him be in the movie. Security mistook the guy for one of the extras. As the intruder became more demanding about being in the movie, Robin said, "He got right up in my face," and with that Robin leaped from his chair into my chair. Eyeball to eyeball with me he continued, "and the guy said 'get me in this movie now!'" Finally Robin got security's attention and the guy was taken away. I was left with Robin practically in my lap reenacting what happened.

ABOVE

During our many interviews, Bruce Willis frequently delighted in teasing me about an imaginary affair we had had.

ABOVE RIGHT

In my 1980 interview with Harrison Ford for *The Empire Strikes Back*, he told me that before he was cast in the starring role of Han Solo in *Star Wars*, he was called in to read for other parts.

Another unpredictable actor was Bruce Willis. His *Armageddon* interview in Los Angeles in 1998 was his wildest performance with me. It was just before he and Demi Moore announced their separation. Every magazine I picked up showed Bruce with his three daughters and praised his commitment to fatherhood. When I mentioned this to him, Bruce said, "Yeah Bobbie, it's not like the old days when you used to come up to the Canyon and we'd dance naked 'til three in the morning."

I quickly shot back, "That was some other Bobbie."

But Bruce carried it on and on. The room producer showed me a one-minute cue and I said, "Okay Bruce, you've used up all my time and there's nothing I can use on the air."

Bruce turned to the producer and said,

"Turn off the clock. I'll decide when she leaves. Now Bobbie, what do you want to ask me?"

Later I was about to start an interview with director Michael Bey when Bruce comes bounding into the room, grabs Bey's microphone and says, "Michael, do you know Bobbie used to come up to the Canyon and we'd dance naked 'til three in the morning?"

Later I asked the crew if Bruce was doing crazy stuff like this in other interviews. And they said, "No. Just yours!"

At the other end of the pole was Harrison Ford. In early *Star Wars* interviews Harrison was cooperative but very soft spoken. And he stared at the floor. I remember one time our chief editor, Tom McDonald, who often edited my pieces, said, "Why don't you get him to look up and speak up?"

LEFT
When director Oliver Stone talked to me in 1986, *Platoon* was a few weeks away from winning Oscars for best picture, director, editing, and sound mixing. Stone wrote and directed the screenplay, which was based on his life-altering experiences during the Vietnam war.

ABOVE
Add author to Bob Hope's long list of career achievements. In 1974, he talked to me about his book *The Last Christmas Show*, his memoir about entertaining military troops all over the world.

OPPOSITE
Bob Hope developed many of his comic characters on the vaudeville stage and on his popular radio show *The Pepsodent Show Starring Bob Hope,* which ran from 1938 until 1948. The success of the 1940 motion picture comedy *Road to Singapore,* the first of seven *Road* films Hope starred in with Bing Crosby, helped to pave the way for his pioneering television career. He hosted the Academy Awards ceremonies thirteen times.

The next time I interviewed Harrison was for the 1984 film, *Indiana Jones and the Temple of Doom.* When I entered the room he was very friendly, but as soon as I began the interview he started looking at the floor. Now what? When I led with the first question I said, "Harrison," and then I stopped. I didn't continue until he looked up and then I rushed to finish the question while he was still looking at me.

Many interviews later he mentioned that we had been "meeting like this" for a long time. I reminded him that he used to stare at the floor. He smiled and said, "I guess I had a foot fetish."

All interviews have their own particular challenges. A case in point is Oliver Stone. My most memorable time with him was for the 1991 film, *JFK.* Oliver knew from previous interviews that I was a Texan and was on the air live the day of the Kennedy assassination. One of the issues I had with *JFK* was that the real Jim Garrison never made the speech Kevin Costner makes at the end of the movie. It was fiction. Stone replied, "I never said I was making a documentary."

My reply to that was, "Then you should give a disclaimer that parts of the film have been changed from what really happened."

He came back, "There is a disclaimer." I said, "Yes, I saw it, but by the time that comes up the audience is in the car halfway home."

When the interview was over and I left the room, I heard a voice calling me. As a woman approached, I thought, if she takes my tapes away from me, I'm going to raise holy hell. But I let her talk. She said, "Oliver sent me to tell you," (I thought, here it comes) "that it was a tough interview, but he admires your guts."

I waited for her to say more, but when she didn't, I said, "Tell Oliver I appreciate his comments and I look forward to our next interview."

Even though Bob Hope never came to our Fort Worth studios, I interviewed him at TCU and other Fort Worth locations. He often said Fort Worth was important to his career because it's where he learned comedy timing. Before his Hollywood days Bob Hope was a vaudeville superstar in New York and Chicago. Bob O'Donnell, head of the Interstate Theater Circuit in Texas, decided to book Hope. Fort Worth's Majestic Theater, which long since has disappeared from Commerce Street, was Hope's first Texas booking, five shows a day. Hope started the first show, but the jokes that were killers in New York and Chicago were getting little or no reaction. So he stepped up the tempo. Talk faster. Punch harder. It wasn't working. What's wrong with these bumpkins? He went back to his dressing room and threw his hat on the table muttering complaints about the stupid audience when he heard a voice in the doorway say, "What's your hurry, Fancy Pants?"

Bob was wearing white trousers and a candy-striped coat. Bob said abruptly, "What?"

The voice repeated, "I said what's your hurry, Fancy Pants?"

Bob said in a sharp tone, "Who are you?"

"I'm Bob O'Donnell, the guy who brought you here. People talk slower here in Texas, so if you'll just slow down, they'll get what you're saying and they'll laugh."

With that, O'Donnell left. Hope was thinking, "Who does he think he is? I'm doing what I did in New York and Chicago and they loved it."

Next show, same thing. Only a few laughs. Finally by the third show, Hope decided to slow down a little bit and he thought he heard more response. By the fourth and fifth shows he slowed down even more and the laughs were much better. In telling me this story Bob said, "It was right here in Fort Worth I learned

about timing and how to play to different audiences."

Bob's favorite audiences were military troops. Every time I was around him, a former serviceman would come up and talk about the time he entertained at their remote camp or base. One time on a long layover at DFW Airport, an American Airlines employee reminded him of a show he did at their camp during World War II. Bob remembered it well, because before the show a young captain came up to him and said that he had been sent by General George Patton to bring Bob to the general's quarters after the show to have dinner. Bob said to the captain, "We've already accepted an invitation to dinner, but tell the General I appreciate his invitation."

The captain persisted. "Mr. Hope, you don't understand. General Patton expects you to have dinner with him tonight." Again Hope said he was sorry, but previous plans made it impossible. The captain made one last attempt. "Mr. Hope," he said, "You don't understand. General Patton sent me here, and he expects me to bring you back to his place for dinner. Now it's your ass or mine." Bob had dinner with Patton.

Bob Hope will forever be linked to the USO as much as he is to show business. He loved to make people laugh, but his power went far beyond laughter. When he died in 2003 at the age of one hundred, President Gerald Ford, Betty Ford, and Nancy Reagan headed the list of dignitaries and stars at his funeral. I was the only media person invited. I was also the only media person included in the salute

ABOVE LEFT
The USO described Bob Hope as their one-man morale machine. Starting with his first show to entertain military troops in 1941 until 1991, he traveled, often in war zones, for the United Services Organizations.

ABOVE
Comedian Johnny Carson debuted as the host of *The Tonight Show* on October 1, 1962.

Betty Buckley took Broadway by storm, landing the role of Martha Jefferson in the musical *1776* on her first day after moving to New York. The show was nominated for seven Tony awards and won three, including best musical.

interview. Because we had planned to use one handheld microphone for Johnny and me to share, we had to do a quick shuffle and have me sit between Johnny and Ed so the three of us could share it. Johnny was beginning to get very nervous about taking Jack Paar's place on *The Tonight Show*. He wanted Ed there for backup in case he ran out of things to say.

From the time ten-year-old Betty Buckley opened her mouth to sing "Steam Heat" from *The Pajama Game*, I knew this Fort Worth girl was headed for Broadway. Twelve years later—in 1969, on her first day in New York—Betty Buckley was cast as Martha Jefferson in the Broadway musical *1776*. By 1983 Buckley had earned a Tony Award for *Cats*. Her singing of "Memory" labeled Buckley "The Voice of Broadway." For her London performance in *Sunset Boulevard*, Betty Buckley was nominated for an Olivier Award. In 2011 she was inducted into the Theater Hall of Fame. Her achievements as an actress and singer include films, television, and concerts as well.

Betty's mother Betty Bob Buckley and I met through journalism contacts and have been close friends for over fifty years. Together, we've attended many of Betty's opening nights in New York, Los Angeles, and London.

Fort Worth's Bill Paxton and I knew about one another, but we never met until Paxton worked with Arnold Schwarzenegger in the 1994 movie *True Lies*. The press trip was at the Four Seasons Hotel in Beverly Hills. Cindy Evans was the producer in charge of Paxton's interviews. The first thing Paxton asked her was, "Is Bobbie Wygant going to interview me?" Cindy assured him I was, but after every interview, he said, "Is Bobbie next?"

Finally Cindy said, "We're moving you up in the rotation. You'll be next."

When she told Bill I was next, he pulled off his microphone and rushed to the door. We nearly collided in the hall, but he picked me up and whirled me around saying, "I've

to Bob later that afternoon at the Academy of Television Arts and Sciences. I sat with Dolores Hope and Phyllis Diller for a three-hour show of performances and tributes by stars from Brooke Shields to Sid Caesar.

Johnny Carson was one of many comedy stars who used Bob Hope as a model for timing. I interviewed Johnny the summer before he took over *The Tonight Show*. He had been engaged by the B'nai B'rith organization to come to Texas to receive its Mr. Wonderful Award. I was to do the interview in Dallas before the event started. Several days earlier I was asked to submit my questions. This had never happened before. The night of the interview we were set up and ready to go when Johnny arrived, but he had Ed McMahon with him and told us that Ed would be joining the

ABOVE
My all-time favorite interview was with Commander James F. Calvert. He was the captain of the nuclear-powered USS *Skate*, which in 1959 was the first submarine to surface through the North Pole's ice cap.

ABOVE
Bill Paxton's costarring role in 1994's action film *True Lies* was the third time director James Cameron cast the Fort Worth native in one of his films. Paxton starred in Cameron's *The Terminator* and *Alien*. The two met while working in the art department at Roger Corman's New World Pictures in the early 1980s.

waited all these years. Finally I'm getting on Bobbie Wygant's show in my hometown Fort Worth, Texas." That was the first of a number of interviews with Bill Paxton. He created an impressive body of work, but he was the most unaffected actor I ever met. Throughout his many years in Hollywood he remained the same guy he was in Fort Worth, Texas, until his untimely death in 2017.

I'm often asked if I have an all-time favorite interview, and I do, but he was not in show business. It's Commander James Calvert. In 1959 Calvert took the nuclear submarine USS *Skate* under the north polar ice cap and surfaced at the North Pole. It was the first time a nuclear submarine had surfaced through the ice. Earlier that year Commander William Anderson took the nuclear sub USS *Nautilus* in and out of the polar ice cap without surfacing. Both missions were highly successful. I read the books of both commanders. When I learned that Calvert was doing a speaking engagement in Fort Worth, I wanted to interview him. As a child I became fascinated with submarines. I think it started with seeing a movie called *Submarine D-1*.

I was not able to reach Calvert until about 9:30 the night before the speech. I explained that I had read his book and wanted very much to interview him. He was polite but said that he was being picked up the next morning at ten o'clock and was leaving as soon as the luncheon was over. I explained that we could pick him up, tape the interview at the studio, and get him back to the hotel by ten o'clock. Then I knew I had to play my trump card. I said that I had read both his book and

Captain Anderson's book and everything Ned Beach ever wrote. Edward "Ned" Beach wrote thirteen books based on his experiences as a submarine commander during World War II. Commander Calvert said, "What time do you want to pick me up in the morning?" I didn't mean to call Beach by his nickname Ned, but I'm sure that's what changed Calvert's mind about doing an interview. He had to know that I really knew something about submarines. When we finished the interview and watched the playback, he was very complimentary and said he was glad he did the interview.

A few years later, when my husband and I were vacationing in Jamaica, I talked us aboard a World War II submarine that had been reconverted for training purposes. The officer of the day gave us a complete tour. I told him about my interview with Commander Calvert. He said, "Is there anything else you'd like to see?"

I said, "Yes, I'd like to see where the men sleep in bunks next to the torpedoes." We stepped inside an area where one sailor was sleeping. My head was twelve inches from his head. I thought, "What if later he told his mates, 'I woke up this morning and this woman was standing next to me'?" They probably would have sent him to a medic for evaluation!

FIFTEEN

The Final Chapter

Add October 1, 2013, to the list of red-letter days in my television career.

OPPOSITE
The new home of KXAS-TV at 4805 Amon Carter Boulevard in Fort Worth is called The Studios at DFW. The 75,000 square foot building is designed to house more than three hundred employees of NBC 5, Telemundo 39, and several businesses associated with NBCUniversal, the parent company of NBC 5.

First was September 29, 1948, when WBAP-TV officially signed on the air to become the first television station in the Southwest. Next was May 16, 1974, when LIN Broadcasting, in a $35 million transaction with Carter Publications, became the new owner of WBAP-TV and, as mandated by the FCC, changed the name to KXAS-TV. Then, in May 1998, NBC purchased KXAS-TV from LIN Broadcasting, and the station added NBC 5 to its KXAS-TV call letters.

That brings us to October 1, 2013, when NBC 5 had the official opening of its new state-of-the-art broadcasting and media facility, located on what was formerly a runway at the long-abandoned Amon Carter Airport. It was a picture-perfect autumn day for the ribbon-cutting ceremony in front of the new building south of Dallas/Fort Worth International Airport. Thomas Ehlmann, president and general manager of NBC 5 KXAS-TV, presided. Mayor Betsy Price gave a Fort Worth welcome to the visiting NBC dignitaries, including Ted Harbert, chairman of NBC Broadcasting, and Valari Staab, president of NBCUniversal Owned Television Stations.

I returned just in time after a summer in France. My trip home was delayed due to an accident I had that resulted in a broken neck bone. I'd spent one week in the American Hospital in Paris.

ABOVE LEFT
President and General Manager of NBC 5 KXAS-TV Thomas Ehlmann had the honor of cutting the ribbon at the grand opening ceremonies of the new facilities on October 1, 2013. Cheering him on were (left to right) KDC Chairman and Chief Executive Steve Van Amburgh, (Ehlmann), Fort Worth Mayor Betsy Price, Telemundo 39 President and General Manager John Trevino, NBCUniversal Chief Executive Officer Steve Burke, and KDC Senior Vice President Bill Guthrey.

ABOVE
Honored guests and corporate dignitaries.

BELOW
NBC 5 news anchors Meredith Land and Brian Curtis gave welcoming remarks.

ABOVE
I took my turn cutting the ribbon, with help from (left to right)
NBC 5 news anchors Brian Curtis, Meredith Land, and Deborah Ferguson;
NBC Arthouse's Tracee Cummins, and NBC 5 Vice Presidents Matt Varney and Brian Hocker.

After the ribbon-cutting ceremony—officially opening the new home of NBC 5 KXAS-TV and Telemundo 39—Tracee Cummins, director of operations NBC Arthouse, took me on a tour of the new facility.

The newsroom is the size of a basketball court. It has wall-to-wall computers. I was amazed to stand inside the front entrance and see clear through the newsroom to the back entrance and back parking lot.

Everyone was waiting to see my reaction to one of the conference rooms dedicated to me. I knew there was such a thing because Brian Hocker, vice president of programming, research, and digital media, had asked me and Erik Clapp, my archivist, to contribute photographs from my archives. I must admit, however, I wasn't prepared for the real thing. There are three conference rooms. A large room dedicated to the station founder, Amon G. Carter Sr. On one side is a room dedicated to the career of Harold Taft, considered the Dean of Television Meteorology. On the other side is the Bobbie Wygant Conference Room, with pictures of me with celebrities and stars I interviewed through the years. I don't know who made the decision to include me, but thank you, thank you. I wish Harold and Mr. Carter were alive to see how they are being honored. I'm not given to false modesty, but I feel like I'm the small boll in a field of tall cotton.

Touring the four studios was a study in contrasts from the original station. The sets are electronic, no canvas-covered flats. The cameras are mostly robotic, but for news programs there is a live floor director.

The new studios have no outside access and are smaller than the main studio in the original building. There won't be any Budweiser horses coming in one door and out the other. Now the cameras go to the horses instead of the horses coming to the TV station.

Looking back on seventy years with this one station is overwhelming in so many ways.

ABOVE
The NBC 5 news anchor desk in the main studio,
one of four in the building.

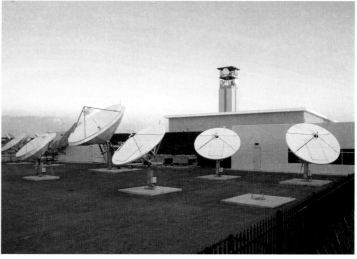

ABOVE
Satellite dishes on the south side of the studios at DFW receive and
transmit from and to more than five hundred different sources.

ABOVE
The interview area in the main NBC 5 studio.

ABOVE
Three high-definition control rooms are supported by a four-thousand-
square-foot data center with five hundred terabytes of storage.

This is the main studio for NBC 5. There are three other studios in the new building.

I'm often asked what it was like being a woman in this industry. With all the opportunities I had as an on-air talk show host, reporter, and producer, working at home base as well as traveling throughout the country and abroad, how can I speak or even think about discrimination as a woman? I think of myself as a very grateful and fortunate broadcaster.

I remember one day in 1977 I was taping my monthly entertainment special, and it suddenly hit me. There were two women operating cameras, Libby Altwegg and Martha Pingel, and in the control room was the director, Carmen Vasquez. I was talent and producer. The sudden realization made me stop and call it to their attention. I said, "Ladies, let's remember this moment." It so impressed me that when I saw a display of small bisque angels in a shop later that day, I bought three and gave one to each of my crew. I called them "My Three Angels." Libby, Martha, and Carmen.

I never once had any sexual harassment. The only discrimination was in pay. During World War II, wages were frozen. When that was lifted in postwar years, the *Star-Telegram* got around to adjusting wages. They took care of the men first. My husband Phil was given a nice raise as well as back pay.

Eventually the women got a raise but no back pay. The women as well as many of the men expressed their opinions that this was unfair. One department head said that the reason women were treated differently was because the company didn't feel they were as good an investment as the men. Women get married and leave or get married and have children and leave. A male employee is a better investment.

LEFT
I'm standing next to one of WBAP-TV's
oldest studio cameras.

ABOVE
On the fiftieth anniversary of the death of President John Kennedy,
NBC 5's Brian Curtis interviewed me about the challenges of
being on the air live as the 1963 events unfolded.

ABOVE
I celebrated my ninetieth birthday on November 22, 2016, with a party of my coworkers at NBC 5, including (from left) meteorologist David Finfrock and NBC 5 news anchors Meredith Land and Brian Curtis.

ABOVE
The City of Fort Worth proclaimed November 22, 2016, as Bobbie Wygant Day. Mayor Betsy Price presented me with the proclamation plaque at my birthday party.

I didn't like the decision but accepted the outcome until I heard about one of the men. He was the security officer who strutted about in his uniform with gun strapped to his side in a fancy holster. He spent most of his time in the reception area watching TV and slurping coffee. When he got his raise and back pay, he couldn't wait to tell everyone. You can imagine how that went over with the women. The joke about him was that if we had an emergency, by the time he put his coffee down and unstrapped his gun he'd probably shoot himself in the foot before he could help anyone in trouble.

While I sometimes wish I had been more aggressive about being better paid, money was never my goal. I never made a six-figure salary. I never had an agent. I wanted work I could enjoy. As I look back over the last seventy years, I have had experiences and travel and have met people from all walks of life who have enriched my life in incalculable ways. I've flown in a T-33 jet trainer and experienced G-forces. I've ridden with troops in an M-48 Patton tank. I've met presidents and three generations of celebrities.

I've survived seventy years in the television business at the same station under three different owners and at least ten different bosses. Except for a couple of dust-ups, I've had good experiences with all of them.

My philosophy has always been I'm here for the long haul. I never aspired to go to New York or Los Angeles. As long as I had good opportunities here, I wanted to live and work in Texas. I want every report to be as good as I know how to make it. I appreciate positive suggestions. I don't play politics. If my work doesn't speak for me, politicking won't help.

Now the big question: after seventy years on the job you might ask, Why are you still "working your buns off"? Answer: I love the work. I love the people. And it keeps me out of bars and Neiman Marcus!

ABOVE
President and General manager of NBC5 KXAS-TV Thomas Ehlmann came aboard in 2009. Our first meeting was a friendly, impromptu encounter in the newsroom. He, like all of the managers I've worked under, encouraged me to keep on keeping on. That's my intention.

TOP LEFT
Lou Diamond Phillips gave me a hug after his opening night performance in *The King and I* at Bass Hall.

ABOVE
I greeted my favorite Texan Tommy Tune at the Dallas Symphony.

ABOVE
Director Blake Edwards and I go back to 1965 when I first interviewed him for *The Great Race*.

TOP RIGHT
Even though I'm officially retired from Channel 5, I'm still out and about talking to stars and filing stories. Betty Bob Buckley (left) and I congratulated Sir Anthony Hopkins when the USA Film Festival saluted him with a Master Screen Artist tribute in 2003.

ABOVE I finally met Yo-Yo Ma, one of my music heroes, at a special gala for the Dallas Symphony.

ABOVE
Every January, I fly to Los Angeles to attend the Critics' Choice Awards. George Pennacchio, entertainment reporter for LA's KABC7, and his wife Erin are my permanent escorts to the formal event every year.

ABOVE CENTER
It was old home week when I stopped by to say hello to actor Richard Chamberlain at the USA Film Festival's salute to him.

ABOVE
I was invited to interview Bradley Cooper for *A Star is Born*, the film he directed and starred in with Lady Gaga. He cowrote the screenplay, wrote some of the songs in the movie, and is also one of the film's producers.

LEFT
Singer-songwriter-actor Lyle Lovett introduced me to his future wife April Kimble when they first got engaged.

LEFT
When I was in London to see Betty Buckley in *Dear World*, an added thrill was having tea with Celia Sandys, granddaughter of Winston Churchill. A Churchill devotee since my teens, I was beyond excited to be talking about my hero with his granddaughter.

Acknowledgments

A huge thank you to all the stars whom I've interviewed over my seventy-year career. Without your interviews I could not have brought you to local audiences or even have written this book. You taught me the great lesson that stars are just people, too.

The photographs in this book represent a fraction of the interviews I've done over the years. Not every interview I did was documented by a still photographer, and as time went on fewer and fewer still photographs were taken. Some priceless photographs unfortunately disappeared, so I am grateful for the ones I still have in my archives. They capture a special moment in time at the dawn of early television and the birth of entertainment journalism.

I started writing copy and scripts as a teenager, so writing the book was not difficult once I researched times, places, and dates. However, writing the manuscript was only the beginning. Fortunately, many people willingly came to my aid. If I've overlooked anyone, I offer sincere apologies. Here are some of the people who made significant contributions.

To Dan Williams, Kathy Walton, Melinda Esco, and their staff at TCU Press, my appreciation and sincere thanks for their expertise, encouragement, and patience. To consultant Nancy McMillen, thanks for her input during the book's initial stages. Thanks also to Diana Carter and Bob Lukeman, who gave new life to aging photographs. And thank you to Bill Brammer for his elegant design.

Special recognition to Channel 5's Bill Glover, in memoriam. Bill took many of the photographs in this book, both in the studio and on location. To Steve Moffett, who directed many of my shows, thank you for saving Bill Glover's photo proofs, and thanks to Barbara Griffith Moffett and Christopher Moffett for assisting Steve.

For photographs and other contributions, thanks to Courtney Jacobs and Gregory Pierce, University of North Texas Libraries, Special Collections; Catherine Spitzenberger, Special Collections, The University of Texas at Arlington Libraries; Mark Davies, The Sixth Floor Museum at Dealey Plaza; and Anne Peterson, DeGolyer Library, Southern Methodist University. Andy Hanson and Bob Jackson, thank you for the fantastic Beatles photographs you took in 1964. I appreciate the extra efforts made by Rachel Lattimore at WBAA, Purdue's radio station in West Lafayette, Indiana; and by Katherine Braz, editor of the *Purdue Alumnus* magazine, to locate the photograph of me on mic in 1945.

To the late *Dallas Morning News* Film Critic Philip Wuntch and his wife Mimi—thank you for inspiring me with Philip's book *Martin Jurow Seein' Stars*, written with film producer Martin Jurow.

Thanks to longtime dear friend and fellow journalist Betty Bob Buckley, who gently but firmly prodded me for ten years to write this book, reminding me that I owed it to my profession. Thanks for the guilt complex, Betty Bob. Thanks also to Ruta Lee, who should write a book on her fascinating life and on how to give informative, fun interviews. And to Michael and Wendy Jenkins, Jo Ann Holt, Durhl Causey, and Paulette Hopkins for help recalling Dallas Summer Musicals shows and stars.

For sharing their personal archives, special thanks to the four children of Frank and Nancy Mills: Marsha Lee Mills Ludlum, David Mills, Gregory Mills, and Clare Mills Hamilton. Their pictures and personal stories provided treasured memories recounted in this book.

From NBC 5 / KXAS-TV, special thanks to Station Manager Tom Ehlmann, News Director Mark Ginther, Brian Hocker, Lauren Wheat, David Finfrock, Tracee Cummins, Libby Altwegg, Carmen Vasquez, Candelaria Vidana, Nada Ruddock, Raul Rangel, Eric Kreindler, Elvira Sakmari, and former newsroom producers Guy Mitchell and Reginald Hardwick. Thanks also to former anchor Russ Bloxom and to retired engineers Robert "Rip" McClendon and I. N. "Red" Walker. Appreciation to photographers Bob Welch and Jimmy Darnell, in memoriam, for their recollections of covering the JFK assassination.

Thank you to Bob Schieffer for encouraging me to write a book and for graciously writing the foreword to *Talking to the Stars.* And Richard Schroeder, thank you for writing your book *Texas Signs On*—I referred to it numerous times while writing this memoir.

Thanks to Roche Madden, the first student I mentored and now a senior reporter for Fox Television News in St. Louis. And to another mentored student, Julia Duffy, who after many years in Hollywood as a comedian has returned to Texas to continue her career. I learned more from the students than I imparted to them.

Appreciation to Olivia Lira, my housekeeper for over thirty years, who has put up with my messy home office overflowing with books, scripts, and lately, material for this book.

To friends of over sixty years who shared the highs and lows of my life: Katherine "Kiki" Smith, Drake Benthall, Colette and Harry Miller, and Shirley and Louis Daniel.

To George Pennacchio, the entertainment guru at KABC-TV in Los Angeles who helped fill in press trip details. When I'm in LA I stay with George and his wife Erin at what we laughingly call the "Pennacchio Bed and Breakfast."

Thank you to Erik Clapp, who came to Channel 5 as an intern and was assigned to "clean up that mess Bobbie calls her archives." Now some twenty years later, Erik is head of EC Films Production Company and is manager of my archives and website. Interviews with many of the stars in this book and numerous others can be seen at www.bobbiewygant.com.

And now for the biggest thank you of all—to Christina Patoski, the photographic editor of this book. Throughout the two years we've been working on *Talking to the Stars* Christina, my longtime friend and former editor at Channel 5, has been my guide, my radar, my most helpful critic. There's no way I can adequately repay her for the months and years of diligent digging to get just the right picture and for the endless hours of making the pictures fit the content. Getting clearances for over five hundred photos was a full-time job, but Christina managed that along with everything else. I shall be eternally grateful to her for her dedication and passion in making this book the best it can possibly be. Without Christina there would be no book. Christina, thank you! Thank you!

I take full responsibility for the written word in *Talking to the Stars.* In spite of checking and double-checking, there may be errors. I hope you readers make allowances for a ninety-plus-year-old memory that may be fuzzy about some details.

After all these years, I still love talking to the stars.

— BW
July 2018

Permissions

Wurts Bros. (New York N.Y.) / Museum of the City of New York. X2010.7.2.7998 - p. X

Everett Collection Historical / Alamy Stock Photo - p. 2 (top)

New York World's Fair 1939-1940 Records, Manuscripts and Archives Division, The New York Public Library, Astor, Lenox and Tilden Foundations - pp. 2 (bottom), 3 (bottom)

Donald C. Larson Collection, Special Collections Research Center, Henry Madden Library, California State University, Fresno - p. 3 (top right)

1939 New York World's Fair, 246468_003_010_001, RCA News and Information Department photographs (Accession 2464.68), Hagley Museum & Library, Wilmington, DE 19807 - p. 3 (top left)

Bettmann/Getty Images - pp. 4 (top right), 36

Courtesy of Purdue University Libraries, Karnes Archives and Special Collections - pp. 8, 13

©KXAS-TV / NBC 5. Used with permission - pp. 20, 21, 23 (left), 26, 29, 30, 37 (left), 46 (top), 47 (middle and right), 52, 53, 55 (top), 57, 58, 59, 60 (top left), 62 (top left, bottom right), 65 (top left, bottom right), 67, 160, 164, 165 (top & bottom right), 166 (left), 170 (bottom), 206, 207, 208, 209, 210 (right), 231, 254, 257 (right), 264, 266 (bottom right), 268, 269, 271, 272

NBC 5 / KXAS (WBAP) Television News Archive, University of North Texas Libraries Special Collections - pp. 22 (right), 23 (right), 28, 31, 32, 35, 37 (top & bottom right), 38, 39, 42, 44, 45, 46 (bottom), 47 (left), 48, 49, 51, 54, 56, 57 (right), 60 (top right), 61, 62, 65 (top right), 66 (left), 70 (right), 71, 72 (top right), 73, 78 (top & bottom left), 83 (top left, top & bottom right), 84 (top right), 87 (bottom right), 88 (top right), 89 (bottom left), 92 (top left), 93 (top right, bottom left), 97 (middle left, bottom right), 98 (top & bottom right), 99, 142 (top left & right), 144 (top & bottom left), 146 (top left & right), 147 (top right), 151 (top right), 152 (top right), 153 (top right), 158 (top & bottom left), 161, 162, 165 (top & bottom right), 168 (right), 169 (right), 170 (top left & right), 171, 172 (left), 174 (top right, bottom left), 180, 185, 206, 207, 229, 232, 255 (top)

Courtesy, Jack White Photograph Collection, Special Collections, University of Texas at Arlington Libraries, Arlington Texas - p. 25

©1949 Time Inc. All rights reserved. Reprinted from LIFE and published with permission of Time Inc. Reproduction in any manner in any language in whole or in part without written permission is prohibited - p. 34

©1953 Broadcast News Magazine, September/October 1953 issue - p. 66 (right)

©1963 Al Panzera - p. 68

©1961 Lee Angle - pp. 74, 75

Courtesy of Steve Moffett - pp. 79 (top right), 81, 91 (top), 95 (left), 140, 145, 146 (bottom), 147 (top left, bottom left & right), 148, 149, 150, 151 (top left, bottom right), 152 (top & bottom left), 153 (top left), 157

Courtesy, Fort Worth Star-Telegram Collection, Special Collections, The University of Texas at Arlington Libraries, Arlington, Texas - pp. 100, 103 (top right, bottom left), 164, 165 (top left)

DeGolyer Library, Southern Methodist University, Andy Hanson Photographs - pp. 102 (top left & right), 110, 112, 114

William Allen, photographer, Dallas Times Herald Collection/The Sixth Floor Museum at Dealey Plaza - pp. 102 (bottom left & right), 103 (top left, bottom right), 107

Dallas Times Herald Collection/The Sixth Floor Museum at Dealey Plaza - pp. 104, 105 (left)

Eamon Kennedy, photographer, Dallas Times Herald Collection/The Sixth Floor Museum at Dealey Plaza - p. 105 (right)

Tom C. Dillard Collection, The Dallas Morning News/ The Sixth Floor Museum at Dealey Plaza - p. 106 (top)

Darryl Heikes, photographer, Dallas Times Herald Collection/The Sixth Floor Museum at Dealey Plaza - p. 106 (bottom)

©1964 Bob Jackson - pp. 113, 115, 117

©1964 The Associated Press - p. 116

Wyoming State Archives - p. 120 (top right)

Courtesy, Warner Bros. Entertainment - pp. 120 (top left), 121, 122, 123, 125

©United Artists. All Rights Reserved. Courtesy Metro-Goldwyn-Mayer Media Licensing - pp. 127, 128, 139

Courtesy, National Archives - pp. 188 (bottom right), 189, 193

Photo by Don Perdue/Courtesy WNET - p. 188 (bottom left)

Courtesy of United States Naval Institute - pp. 190, 192

Photo by Jim Frost. Courtesy of Sun-Times Media Productions, LLC - p. 191

©1965 Twentieth Century-Fox. All Rights Reserved - p. 196

©Paramount/Courtesy Everett Collection - p. 217 (left)

©1982 Universal City Studios, Inc. All Rights Reserved. Courtesy ITV/REX/Shutterstock - p. 217 (right)

Courtesy of Universal Studios Licensing LLC - pp. 218, 219

ZUMA Press, Inc. / Alamy Stock Photo - p. 239

©2018 The Dallas Morning News - p. 240

Courtesy of Libby Martelle - p. 242 (bottom), 243, 252

©Christina Patoski - pp. 246, 274 (top left)

©2003 Glen Ellman - p. 247

Courtesy of Richard Kaufman - p. 249

Tsuni / USA / Alamy Stock Photo - p. 257 (left)

Photo by Martha Swope ©Billy Rose Theatre Division, The New York Public Library for the Performing Arts - p. 261

Photo by Zade Rosenthal ©1994 Twentieth Century-Fox. All Rights Reserved - p. 262

Courtesy, Naval History & Heritage Command - p. 262 (right)

©2013 Erik Clapp - pp. 266 (top & bottom left, top right), 267, 270, 275

Courtesy of the USA Film Festival - pp. 273 (top left, bottom middle), 274 (top right)

All other photographs are from the author's collection

Index

BW = Bobbie Wygant